SHEKINAH

Appreciating the manifested glory of God

HELIO NESPOLI

SHEKINAH: APPRECIATING THE MANIFESTED GLORY OF GOD

This book is written to provide information and motivation to readers. Its purpose is not to render any type of psychological, legal, or professional advice of any kind. The content is the sole opinion and expression of the author, and not necessarily that of the publisher.

Copyright © 2019 by Helio Nespoli

All rights reserved. No part of this book may be reproduced, transmitted, or distributed in any form by any means, including, but not limited to, recording, photocopying, or taking screenshots of parts of the book, without prior written permission from the author or the publisher. Brief quotations for noncommercial purposes, such as book reviews, permitted by Fair Use of the U.S. Copyright Law, are allowed without written permissions, as long as such quotations do not cause damage to the book's commercial value. For permissions, write to the publisher, whose address is stated below.

All scripture quotations and verses used in this book are taken from the New King James translation, whose copyrights belong to Thomas Nelson/ HarperCollins Christian Publishing and fit under their Gratis Use Guidelines, not requiring permission to be used, according to their site (https:// www.thomasnelson.com/about-us/permissions/) on 06/16/2019.

Printed in the United States of America.

ISBN   978-1-64552-068-9   (Paperback)
ISBN   978-1-64552-069-6   (Digital)

Library of Congress Cataloging-in-Publication Data
Names: Nespoli, Helio, author
Title: Shekinah: Appreciating the Manifested Glory of God
Publisher: Lettra Press LLC - 18229 E 52nd Ave. - Denver City, CO 80249 - 1 303 586 1431 |
info@lettrapress.com
www.lettrapress.com

This book may be ordered through booksellers or by contacting:

SHEKINAHNOW
www.shekinahnow.com
5500 Lavon dr
Garland, TX 75040
1 469 974 4955 | info@shekinahnow.com

CONTENTS

Dedication vii
Endorsements ix
Background xiii
Introduction xv

Chapter 1: Understanding the New Birth 1
Chapter 2: The Daily Devotional 7
Chapter 3: Praise/Adoration 13
Chapter 4: 1st Requirement – Boldness 19
Chapter 5: 2nd Requirement – Through the Blood of Jesus 23
Chapter 6: 3rd Requirement – By The New And Living Way 27
Chapter 7: 4th Requirement – A True Heart 33
Chapter 8: 5th Requirement – Full Assurance of Faith 37
Chapter 9: 6th Requirement – A Heart Cleansed from A
            Bad Conscience 55
Chapter 10: 7th Requirement – The Body Washed with
            Clean Water 63
Chapter 11: Summary of the Requirements to
            Enter the Holy of Holies 69

Final Words 75
About the Author 77

DEDICATION

I dedicate this work, first of all, to my Lord Jesus Christ for his sacrifice and death and for having called me to be a minister of the gospel, which is what I love to do: teaching, ministering the Word and helping others.

I also dedicate this book to my wife, Silvia, a gift from God to me since 1982, who has dedicated her love, care and attention to me, who God has placed by my side to minister and work with me and who has motivated and supported me all these years. I declare my love, admiration and respect for her and her example as a wife, mother, daughter-in-law, daughter, leader and woman of God.

I also wish to dedicate this book to my dear children: Gian Marcelo, Pietro Luigi and Mirella Raquel, who God gave me the privilege of having, and who have brought me, much happiness and satisfaction through their special lives, as well as those of their spouses.

I must not forget to mention my grandmother Mina, who always prayed for me and who was responsible for insisting that we have an evangelical education, which was the basis for my conversion in 1974.

I would also like to express my sincere thanks and admiration for my beloved parents and my in-laws for the education and example of character, honor and work they provided for me and for all the love, effort and patience they showed me.

I would like to express my gratitude to God for Pastor Walter Rodrigues and his wife, my beloved aunt Cleide, and for having been tremendously used by God in our lives.

I would like to express my admiration, love and gratitude for the life of Pastor Coty (Marcos de Souza Borges), for his character and for the very important work he has developed and ministered in the areas of healing, deliverance and teaching, which has strongly impacted our lives and the body of Christ both in Brazil and other parts of the world.

I wish to express my admiration and respect for Pastor E. Wayne Hanks. His vision and compassion for people goes out of the boundaries of the church he has dedicated his whole life to: First at Firewheel (Garland First Assembly of God). Since our arrival to the US in 1989, Pastor Hanks and his wife have been so loving and caring for my family, not only by words, but by actions. My admiration for your character, testimony and steadfastness will be always engraved in my heart and mind with a sincere attitude of thankfulness.

ENDORSEMENTS

It has been wisely noted that, "Many people want more 'from' God instead of more 'of' God." If you desire more 'of' God, hungering and thirsting for His righteousness, then I am sincerely grateful for the opportunity to recommend this anointed resource to you in your pursuit. I truly believe that Appreciating SHEKINAH, The Manifested Glory of God, was written from a heart that passionately yearns for the abiding presence of our Heavenly Father. Here Pastor Helio Vassão Nespoli sets forth clear guidelines for those who desire to go deeper with God.

Having the privilege to know the author since 1988, when he and his family became members of our church family, I can witness to the fact that he writes not only from his theological training, but from personal experience as well. Through his numerous personal challenges and vicissitudes, I have also been inspired by observing a constant faithfulness and love for God and His Kingdom in both Pastor Helio and his wife Silvia. More than hollow rhetoric, he shares from the crucible of his own life in a manner that exalts Christ, illuminates the Scriptures, and encourages the reader to obediently step into a practical application of divine realities. Outlining helpful steps for developing and maintaining a strong devotional life, cultivating the privilege and power of prayer, safeguarding vital relationships, and freely offering anointed worship which leads one into the 'holy of holies,' are just some of the dimensions to be explored.

With confidence I can say that your genuine desire to walk closer to the Lord will be encouraged, strengthened, and rewarded as you read this book. By following its principles, you are assured of this promise from Jesus: "Blessed are those who hunger and thirst for righteousness, for they shall be satisfied." (Matthew 5:6 RSV)

Pastor E. Wayne Hanks

Lead Pastor, First at Firewheel Church, Garland, Texas

General Presbyter, North Texas District Assemblies of God

- Rev. Dr. Helio V Nespoli has presented us a wonderful book full of practical lessons for victory in our lives. It contains Scriptural references that brings the content into something you know will work. There are many books that are written with much theory and speculation attached, but this book is very authentic, and has a lot of his personal life experiences interwoven that you can see that his journey has accomplished victory for him. Dr. Nespoli is a student of the Word, and I invite you to share this publication with as many of your friends as you can.

Sincerely yours in Christ,

D. Leland Paris

Founder / Director Youth With A Mission Tyler, Texas

- Adoration isn't a gift for some people, but a calling for everyone. I hope the content of this book will guide the readers by the wings of the Spirit and truth to the highest places and intimacy with God. I recommend not just this book, but also his author, Pastor Helio, a dear friend and colleague in ministry.

Pr. Marcos de Souza Borges (Coty) – International speaker, missionary since 1986 at YWAM (Youth With A Mission) in Brazil, author of 11 books, where one of them is a best seller (Intelligent Shepherding), founder and creator of EIFOL (Integral School for training of Deliverers), a seminar that has impacted and trained thousands of leaders in Brazil and internationally in the inner healing and deliverance ministry.

- Having personally known Helio Nespoli and his wife, Silvia, for many years and observing their perseverance and dedication to their calling, I would gladly recommend his new book, The Shekinah, to all readers. Definitely the only place to truly learn from God, and become more Christlike, is in His presence. Many would like to experience His presence but, at the same time, are hesitant for fear or are uninformed on how to enter this holy place. I believe that this book would well serve to guide the sincere and hungry souls to a much greater intimacy with God, as well as growing spiritual victory.

Thomas L. Wilkins

Missionary, church planter and pastor in Brazil for 52 years; member of Ministers Fellowship International and currently ministering to pastors in the greater São Paulo, Brazil.

- Pastor Helio Vassão Nespoli, as the result of the calling of God in his life, brings to light this book, through which he manifests his unshakeable faith in the Word of God and purposes to take us from our comfort zone and lead us to seek and attain the perfecting of the Saints by entering into the Most Holy Place. I congratulate the author for the brilliant and faithful manner exposed in this work, containing ideas enriched by the clear revelations of God to his spirit. I believe the outreach of this book will be great, especially among those who seek to have a life of intimacy with God. I wish that the reader be fed by the substance of the divine truths contained in this book, and that their spirit be strengthened by the nutrients of the sap of virtue, so that it may reinvigorate their conscience with respect to the responsibilities of the duty inherent to all who profess the lordship of Christ in their lives.

Pastor Antonio Carlos Cerruti Bernardes de Oliveira, BA., MBA., MTH. BS., DD., PhD. International Lecturer, Founder and President of the Casa do Oleiro Apostolic International Ministries, with head offices in Dallas, TX, USA, who has performed a great apostolic work involving the planting of churches, schools, daycares and community centers in various countries, especially those with greater needs, such as Russia, Brazil, Japan, India and several African countries.

- I have the privilege of recommending this book to any reader and to those who love the Word of God. In a very objective and anointed way, Pastor Helio Vassão Nespoli records his experience with the principles of the Divine Word through the revelations of the Holy Spirit. It is pure teaching of one of the believer's greatest privileges in Jesus Christ: to enter into the Holy of Holies. All those who wish to hear the voice of God must come near him. Every reader of this book will understand the meaning of the title given to it, for it is truly "the greatest experience of worship a human being can have". God bless all in the reading and meditation of the teachings of this book.

Pastor Helio Haroldo de Souza Rodrigues – Pastor Leader of the Intercultural Ministry at First Assembly of God at Firewheel in Garland, TX, USA, Chaplain Master and founder of OUSAC (Oneword USA Chaplaincy), Architect, President of Oneword Development, Inc. (Dallas-TX). Pastor since 1984.

BACKGROUND

Born in an evangelical home in 1959, Hélio Vassão Nespoli had a real encounter with the Lord Jesus at age 15, on 11/01/1974.

He has been married to Silvia since 1982, with whom he has 3 adult children. He was ordained pastor in 1985 and founded and pastored churches in Brazil and the USA until 2012. He had a secular job as an animal dentist, specialized in large animals, from 1981 through 1997, mainly treating horses and correcting their bytes with braces all over Brazil and later the USA. Later was accredited by the State of Florida as a "business broker" (professional specializing in the sales of companies). He brought American investment funds to Brazil (including Harvard University's endowment fund and Prudential Insurance Company). Helio attended the Florida Theological Seminary in Orlando, Florida (currently known as the Florida Christian University), where he received his Bachelor's, Masters and Doctorate degrees, and where he also taught both in Portuguese and English at the time when Dr. Harold L. Shindoll was its president. Pastor Helio also created the REDIMA Seminar (REsgatando a DIgnidade Masculina – Redeeming the Male Dignity), where he ministers to men about returning to the original principles of God and how to attain God's purpose for their lives. At the same time, his wife, Pastor Silvia, ministers the REVIVA to the women (REcuperando uma VIda de Valor – Recovering a Worthy Life), addressing the various challenges women face and how to live a life satisfied in God. As a couple, Pastors Hélio and Silvia also minister a seminar entitled IN LOVE I and II for couples both in churches of various denominations as well as in other organizations, where the spiritual and relational bases that God created for the couple and the home are ministered by both pastors. With matrimonial experience since 1982, plus the 5-1/2 years of courtship, there is an experience and journey with God that is being shared with the body of Christ. Pastors Helio and Silvia are also part of Pastor Marcos de Souza Borges' (Coty) team, who is the national director of JOCUM (Jovens Com Uma Missão – YWAM -Youth with a Mission), ministering and teaching on healing and deliverance at EIFOL Escola Integral de Formação de Libertadores – "Complete School of Deliverance Training"). The couple resides in Dallas area, Texas, in the USA, where they develop their ministry through seminars and the advertising of Pastor Coty's books and EIFOL, both in Portuguese, Spanish and English. Pastors Helio and Silvia are also establishing a church to reach out to the Brazilian and Portuguese speaking people. Pr. Nespoli was invited to teach in English for the American men of the church in regards to inner healing and deliverance, which is happening once a week at First at Firewheel in Garland. Also, the Nespolis assist pastors that are counseling people in need of emotional healing, understanding that the vision of the church that was established by Jesus is to restore the person fully: spirit, soul, body and all the aspects of life.

INTRODUCTION

The most wonderful, sublime and extraordinary being in the entire universe and of all times is the person of God. If we think about someone who is pure love and at the same time has supreme authority, glorious majesty and absolute power, this is the sovereign God who was, is and will always be the same; *"with whom there is no variation or shadow of turning"*, according to James 1:17.

In spite of God being omnipresent (being everywhere), His glory is only manifested in some instances and to few people.

This glory is known as "Shekinah", which means "the glory of God revealed, expressed or manifested". The word "Shekinah" isn't in the bible, but it has the same meaning as the word "doxa" {the unspoken manifestation of God and His splendor). It was used commonly by the Jews and early Christians.

Between the fall of man in the garden of Eden and the death of the Lord Jesus, the Shekinah was manifested relatively few times, it is very strong, powerful and holy. That's why only men with a specific call from God, prepared by Him and in places chosen by God were able to experience and "endure" it, as in the case of Moses on the Mount, according to Hebrews 12:21:

"And so terrifying was the sight that Moses said, "I am exceedingly afraid and trembling."".

God always wanted to be with man and have a relationship with him. The evidence of this is that, in order to be present with his people in the desert, He ordered that they make Him a sanctuary, in accordance with Exodus 25:8:

"And let them make Me a sanctuary, that I may dwell among them".

Below is a schematic drawing of the sanctuary the Lord had them build and the holy of hollies:

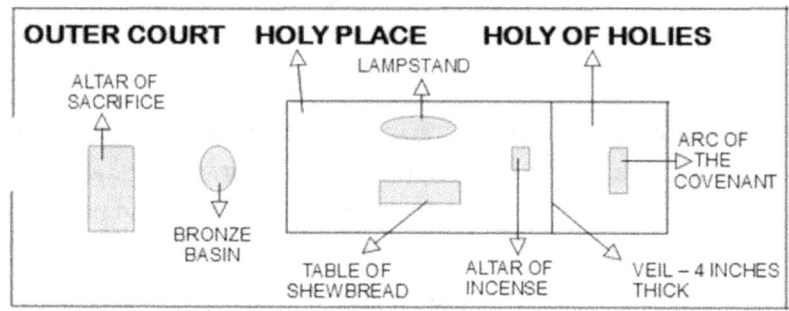

The Shekinah is what filled this sanctuary, in accordance with Exodus 40:34 and 35:

*"Then the cloud covered the tabernacle of meeting, and the glory of the Lord (the SHEKINAH) filled the tabernacle. And Moses was not able to enter the tabernacle of meeting, because the cloud rested above it, and the **glory of the Lord filled the tabernacle**".*

Inside the sanctuary, God established a special place called the holy of holies, or the most holy place, where only the high priest could enter once a year and only after being fully purified and prepared to enter therein. The holy of holies was a distinct place, delimited by walls and a veil 4 inches thick, that is, it was an area set apart and defined for the specific purpose of ministering to the Lord.

When Jesus was on the cross, the veil that separated the sanctuary from the holy of holies was torn, giving access to the Shekinah by all, according to Mark 15:38:

"Then the veil of the temple was torn in two from top to bottom".

The Shekinah is the glory of God; it is like seeing the light of his face shining all of its splendor, grace, love and power.

Whoever experiences the Shekinah, comes to the conclusion that there is no greater or more satisfying experience than to experience it, for it is so beautiful and magnificent that it brings forth a joy and peace that cannot be compared to any other imaginable experience.

Unfortunately, the vast majority of people do not seek God. Many do not seek Him because they associate the image of God with that of their natural father or a figure of male authority with whom they grew up. In our childhood, the majority of people sense that, if their father is sad, happy, upset or unhappy with something we did and we end up associating this with the celestial father. Also, many are those who "use" the person of God as someone "angry" who is going to punish the child for having done something wrong or if the child misbehaves, by saying: "look, the heavenly father is going to punish you...". This ends up forming an association between the "earthly father" and the "heavenly father", producing a great distortion of who God really is. This creates a few stereotypes in the minds of people. It generates mistakes such as: if the person had an austere and disciplinary father, he/she believes that God is a grumpy old man who is waiting for the individual to do something wrong in order to punish him. If the person had a liberal father, he/she thinks that God is that same way, that He doesn't care, who will allow the child to do whatever he/she wants. If the individual was raised receiving many presents and toys, he believes that God is some kind of Santa Claus, who will give all he/she asks for and make all wishes come true.

Regardless of whether the earthly father was a wonderful person or even an example as a father, such earthly father is far from being compared to the person of God and his personality.

It is very important to dissociate, to disconnect the figure of your earthly father from God. Only then will you be able to know who He really is and be marveled by His admirable characteristics.

God declared the following through the prophet Hosea, chapter 4:6:

"My people are destroyed for lack of knowledge. Because you have rejected knowledge, I also will reject you from being priest for Me; Because you have forgotten the law of your God, I also will forget your children".

The lack of knowledge leads to destruction. The prophet was referring to the knowledge of God, since on chapter 6, verse 3, he declares:

"Let us know, let us pursue the knowledge of the Lord. His going forth is established as the morning; He will come to us like the rain, Like the latter and former rain to the earth".

If you determine in your heart to know God without the stereotypes, sophisms and paradigms created in your mind with respect to Him, and disconnect from pre-conceived ideas you might have concerning God, you will see that this is not only an extraordinary experience, but you will marvel at the splendor and exuberance of the glory of God, with all the glorious characteristics of His personality.

Those who love God and thirst after his presence in their lives, love to get closer to the light, according to John 3:19 through 21:

"And this is the condemnation, that the light has come into the world, and men loved darkness rather than light, because their deeds were evil. For everyone practicing evil hates the light and does not come to the light, lest his deeds should be exposed. **But he who does the truth comes to the light, that his deeds may be clearly seen, that they have been done in God".**

Do you really know God?

Do you wish to experience something you never imagined was possible, something that cannot be compared to anything you have lived, heard or seen to this date? If you know Him, do you want to go deeper in your relationship with Him?

Do you wish to fulfill that void inside of you that thirsts for more of God?

Do you want to have answers to the doubts and anxieties that are deep inside of you, those things you have never expressed to anyone and that only God knows? To understand the meaning of life and have a broader vision and see things that are beyond what your eyes and ears can perceive?

When you experience Shekinah, the light of God shines in your life, you have a clearer understanding and things take on a different and sublime meaning. As your priorities change, your life takes on a new path which brings you into alignment with the center of God's will and your problems seem to diminish.

The Shekinah cannot be detached from God, it is part of Himself and can be manifested wherever God so determines, but there is a place determined by God, where He will always manifest the Shekinah, which is in the holy of holies.

Today, this place is no longer physical, but it is open to whoever wishes to enter into it. Chapter 10 of the book of Hebrews 19 through 22, describes the steps we should take to enter into this extraordinary place.

It is the desire to adore God that leads us to enter into the holy of holies and to experience the Shekinah.

This marvelous experience is what we will express in this book, because this glorious experience will certainly bring a new outlook on life, enabling a higher level of communion with God never before attained and transform the lives of those who experience it.

May God bless you abundantly not only in this reading, but also in the practice of entering into the holy of holies, to adore God, and to experience Shekinah!

CHAPTER 1
Understanding the New Birth

When Jesus says in John 4:23 and 24: *"but the hour is coming"*, and follows it with: **and now is"**, He is establishing something there that did not exist before. The remainder of the verses say:

"...when the true worshipers will worship the Father in spirit and truth; for the Father is seeking such to worship Him. God is Spirit, and those who worship Him must worship in spirit and truth".

Before Jesus spoke this word, it was not possible for someone to worship the Father in spirit because no one had the opportunity of the new birth and Jesus was the only son who came to the world, that is, the **only Begotten,** according to John 3:16:

"For God so loved the world that He gave His only begotten Son, that whoever believes in Him should not perish but have everlasting life".

This is explained in more detail when God said to Adam in Genesis 2:17:

*"...but of the tree of the knowledge of good and evil you shall not eat, for in the day that you eat of it **you shall surely die**".*

We know the facts and we know that Eve ate of the fruit and also gave it to Adam to eat and the word of God was fulfilled, that is, they died, but continued to "live", that is, eating, drinking, walking, talking, breathing, having emotions, etc. What kind of death was this, then? It was the death of the spirit of man, even though the spirit was still inside of him.

As of the death of the spirit, people began to live at the level of the soul and the body, but their spirits had no life. The original word that characterizes the soul is the greek word "$\psi\upsilon\chi\eta$" which corresponds to the word "psych" and occurs in one form or another approximately 755 times in the old and 105 times in the new testament. It is from the word "psych" that the word "psychology" was formed (psych = soul + logy = study, that is: psychology = study of the soul).

The soul encompasses our emotions (and feelings), reasoning (and thoughts) and will. It is influenced by the circumstances, especially by what we see and hear, and has a strong tendency to worry and be anxious, many times being dominated by these two feelings.

Jesus spoke about something that had never before been mentioned in the entire bible until then: the **"new birth"**, in John 3, telling about it to Nicodemus, who was a religious man, but did not seem to understand what Jesus was talking about, interpreting such **"new birth"** as being a physical birth.

It is clear, however, that God did not conceive any son before Jesus came to the world, otherwise Jesus would not have been His ONLY BEGOTTEN SON, but rather His third, tenth, thousandth, etc.

Jesus went from being the "only begotten" to "first", that is, from the "only one" to the "first one", because after him many were born again and became children, according to John 1:11 through 13:

"He came to His own, and His own did not receive Him. But as many as received Him, to them He gave the right to become children of God, to those who believe in His name: who were born, not of blood, nor of the will of the flesh, nor of the will of man, but of God".

This demonstrates that in the old covenant there was no way to worship God as the Father and in "spirit" and in "truth" by anyone.

It was through a conversation I had with a Jewish rabbi that I was able to understand the reason why the Jews would get so irritated when Jesus would declare to be the Son of God.

The Jews understand that men are creatures of God, including Abraham, David, Isaiah, that is, all individuals after Adam. Therefore, we can understand why they were so opposed to Jesus, according to John 19:7:

*"The Jews answered him, "We have a law, and according to our law He ought to die, **because He made Himself the Son of God**".*

When the Father manifested Himself after the baptism of Jesus, He clearly declared that Jesus was "The" beloved son, according to Matthew 17:5:

*"While he was still speaking, behold, a bright cloud overshadowed them; and suddenly a voice came out of the cloud, saying, "This is **My** beloved Son, in whom I am well pleased. Hear Him!"*

David expressed in Psalm 103:1:

"Bless the Lord, O my soul; And all that is within me, bless His holy name! Bless the Lord, O my soul, And forget not all His benefits".

He could not have said, "bless the Lord, O my spirit", because since he had not been born again and this could not have taken place prior to the coming of Jesus, he could not have blessed the Lord this way. This was the highest form he could achieve, blessing the Lord with his soul.

The fact that today we have the opportunity of being children of God is so wonderful and celebrated among the brethren of the new testament, that John wrote about it in I John 3:1:

"Behold what manner of love the Father has bestowed on us, that we should be called children of God! Therefore the world does not know us, because it did not know Him".

This verse demonstrates the joy and the privilege God has given us through Christ of being his children, which did not exist prior to his coming, the shedding of his blood, his death and resurrection.

Now we have the greatest privilege that a human being can have, which is to born again through receiving Christ, according to John 1:12. After this happens, the great privilege of entering into a spiritual place where Jesus was the first to enter, according to Hebrews 6:19 and 20 is possible:

"This hope we have as an anchor of the soul, both sure and steadfast, and which enters the Presence behind the veil, where the forerunner has entered for us, even Jesus, having become High Priest forever according to the order of Melchizedek".

The adoration in the holy of holies, together with the experience of the Shekinah that is manifested there, is an open opportunity for all those who are born again, (had their spirit renewed), something that had never been practiced before Jesus, but is what the Father is seeking. Certainly, those who adore in this fashion do so in spirit and in truth, if they have prepared themselves for this, by complying with the requirements for entering in this place, as described in Hebrews.

If you have not had this marvelous and vital experience of being born again, make this decision now! Say a prayer delivering your life to God, inviting the Lord Jesus to live within you. In accordance to John 1:12, if you receive Christ in your life, you will become a child of God by faith, in accordance with Ephesians 2:8 and 9:

"For by grace you have been saved through faith, and that not of yourselves; it is the gift of God, not of works, lest anyone should boast";

Romans 10:9 also says:

"...that if you confess with your mouth the Lord Jesus and believe in your heart that God has raised Him from the dead, you will be saved".

Jesus only enters in a heart that invites Him to enter. The following prayer serves as a model of invitation (if you wish to pray this way, do so in an audible voice):

"Lord Jesus Christ, I believe that you came to this world, manifested in the flesh and shedding your pure blood to save me. I now receive you as my Lord and my Savior, according to your word, which says that all those who receive you become a child of God. Wash me with your blood and forgive me of my sins. I ask you to come and live within me permanently, controlling and directing my life as my Lord. I want to serve and obey you for the rest of my days. Write my name in the book of life. Amen".

CHAPTER 2
The Daily Devotional

There is a big difference between a hunch, a suggestion, an opinion, an advice and a commandment. Jesus affirmed in Matthew 6:6:

"But you, when you pray, go into your room, and when you have shut your door, pray to your Father who is in the secret place; and your Father, who sees in secret, will reward you openly".

What Jesus was talking about was not a hunch, suggestion, opinion or advice, but rather a commandment! This means that if we don't practice it, it will be the same as not practicing any other commandment of Jesus, that is, disobeying him and suffering the consequences of such disobedience.

The devotional is in an intimate place; it is not a car, street, school, bus, etc. This does not mean that we should not pray in those places, because the bible teaches that we must pray everywhere (I Timothy 2:8). However, what Jesus is referring to here is that we should pray in a specific place because it is there where we will find intimacy with the Father. When He says, shutting "your" door, it means that we need to define the territory and place boundaries so that everything that is outside of it remains outside and does not invade our privacy!

The original word for room here is "tameion", which means "an inner chamber", translated in other versions as: inner room, closet, private room, chamber. In essence, it defines a place of intimacy, a territory, an environment that defines and sets the boundary as to what is "inside" from what is "outside", which means that inside is just the Father and me and outside is everything else, even things and situations pertaining to my life. At first, this understanding seems obvious, but it is important so that we know that God establishes and respects territories ("topos", in the original). Just as an individual is a territory, a house is a territory, an inner chamber is also a territory (I use my bedroom as my "inner chamber"), which is of the greatest intimacy in the life of an individual, where there are no masks, where we take our clothes off, where the deepest secrets are revealed and it is where we can also relax and rest.

It is in the inner room where we can enter into a type of spiritual isolation, after we shut "our door", without the distractions of the daily routine, where we will have communion with the Father and the Father with us.

This is the greatest opportunity we have to enter in the holy of holies and experience the encountering with the Shekinah! There are no distractions, "our" door is closed; there are no worries as to what others are thinking, wearing, saying or doing. The bills, responsibilities and obligations have stayed outside; the world and all the worries stayed outside; you are here, you and God your Father and that is it!

What happens when we first wake up? The first thing that comes to our mind is this question: what do I have to do today? At the same time, our mind starts to process a multitude of information concerning commitments, obligations, phone calls, emails, messages, etc., that is, tasks we need to perform which, in the majority of the cases, lead us to start experiencing what our soul has a huge tendency to experience: anxiety and worry. The greatest majority of people reach for their smart phones right away to check their messages, what is going on in the social medias as well as the latest news! The problem is that these things excite and agitate us to such an extent, especially due to the number of things we have to do, that ultimately we convince ourselves that devotional is a waste of energy and we do not have time for it.

However, there is something very important that must be done so that we do not find our soul keep demanding, questioning and influencing us, which is founded in Psalm 131:2:

"Surely I have calmed and quieted my soul, like a weaned child with his mother; Like a weaned child is my soul within me".

This means that, as a child is to its mother, so is our soul to us, that is, it keeps on "sucking" our strength and energy and needs to be "weaned".

Sucking means: demanding, depending, getting, etc. This is one of the greatest challenges I personally face in my life: to calm and quiet my soul when I am praying in my bedroom. Until this happens, my soul keeps on bringing obligations, doubts, anxiety, restlessness, worries, unbelief, uncertainties, questionings, in other words, all that can take away my concentration.

When we "wean" our soul, that is, when our soul is calmed and quieted it is when our spirit can be released so we can enter into a marvelous dimension. This is also when we have the opportunity to enter into the holy of holies, to worship God in spirit and in truth and to experience the Shekinah. It is the greatest, most glorious and sublime experience that the human being can have in adoration.

Psalm 5:3 says:

"My voice You shall hear in the morning, O LORD; in the morning I will direct it to you, and I will look up".

It is in the morning that we prepare ourselves to face the day ahead which, most certainly, will be full of events, demands, situations, challenges and circumstances. This will require of us, regardless of the environment in which we live: decisions, reactions, postures, answers and thoughts that have the potential to bring us victories, achievements and progress, but that could also bring us hurts, frustrations, sadness and defeats. That is why it is so important to do the devotional in the morning and calm and quiet the soul (emotions and thoughts), so that we may attain the peace, calmness and serenity we need in order to have fellowship with our wonderful Father and face the day ahead of us.

Anxiety and worry not only take us away from the goal, but create pressure, which is what hinder us the most, mainly when it is time for us to make decisions and resolve problems.

A practical example of this is recorded in Luke 10:38-42:

"Now it happened as they went that He entered a certain village; and a certain woman named Martha welcomed Him into her house. And she had a sister called Mary, who also sat at Jesus' feet and heard His word. But Martha was <u>distracted</u> with much serving, and she approached Him and said, "Lord, do You not care that my sister has left me to serve alone? Therefore tell her to help me." And Jesus answered and said to her, "Martha, Martha, you are <u>worried and troubled</u> about many things. But one thing is needed, and Mary <u>has chosen</u> that good part, which will not be taken away from her."

Jesus is not condemning whoever works or occupies him/herself with the tasks needed to be done; He is clearly dealing with what is more important, what is the priority. He said that Mary has chosen the **good part**, which would not be taken away from her.

It is only when we choose the good part that we have access to what is recorded in the book of Psalms 23:5, where the Bible tells us:

"You prepare a table before me in the presence of my enemies: you anoint my head with oil; my cup runs over".

This table that David mentions is what God prepares for us every day so that we may help ourselves to it. At the time David lived, he did not have a complete table like we have today, because we live under the new covenant, which, according to Hebrews 8:6 it is not only better but is also grounded on better promises.

That table is the table of the children and was mentioned in Matthew *15:26 and 27* by Jesus to the Canaanite woman:

"...But He answered and said, "It is not good to take the children's bread and throw it to the little dogs." And she said, "Yes, Lord, yet even the little dogs eat the crumbs which fall from their masters' table."

That table contains what is described in the book of Ephesians 1:3:

"Blessed be the God and Father of our Lord Jesus Christ, who has blessed us with every spiritual blessing in the heavenly places in Christ".

God has served us at that table with all that we need. Note that the verb "blessed" is in the past tense. So, the table is served….

All spiritual blessings are all the achievements and victories that Jesus attained for us through His life, death and resurrection.

I leave as a testimony that, I do not know if I would have been able to face the many challenges, temptations, trials and difficulties that I have faced in my life (including colon cancer in 2011), had it not been for the daily practice of the devotional time in my life since 1992. I also certainly would not have had the experiences, victories, achievements, emotional healing, growth, directives, deliverances, and the manifestation of the grace of God that I have experienced in my life if I was not practicing the daily devotional.

Having a devotional time is the basis, the spiritual oxygen that we need, to develop a relationship, fellowship and communion with the Father.

Purpose in your heart to practice this habit daily, investing time with God. Know that He will fulfill that which he promised at the end of the verse:

*"...and your Father, who sees in secret, will **reward you openly".***

This shows that the success and the blessing of God in our lives are directly related to the relationship we develop with Him in our place of intimacy, our "inner chamber".

True priorities are not those we say we have, but rather those where we truly invest our time and attention to. First importance isn't when an individual agrees or says that seeking God and practicing the daily devotional is important, if the first thing he/she does in the morning is to allow anxiety and worries to take over the soul. Also, it's not by giving priority to social medias, messages, SMS, twitter, blogs, instagram, TV, news, etc., and running out the door to meet the daily activities instead of spending time with the Lord, when he/she would be calming and quieting the soul and strengthening the spirit. Beyond disobeying the Lord, this creates the risk of falling into temptations, making wrong decisions, becoming stressed, overloaded with cares and uncertainties, also trying to fulfil the demands (sucking) of the soul, etc.

Make a commitment to practice every day the devotional and you will see not just the situation changing, but your spirit will be strengthened and you will be able to practice the will of God, doing the 3 most important actions a person should do every day, which are:

1. Living and walking in the spirit, (Romans 8, Galatians 5);
2. Crucifying your flesh with its passions and desires, (Luke 9:23, Galatians 5); and
3. Having your soul restored by the renewing of your mind, (Romans 12:2)

CHAPTER 3
Praise/Adoration

We were born and created by God to have a relationship with Him. Since the creation, God's wish was to have communion and an intimate relationship with man. This was shown through the lives of the men who were called by God to receive the revelation of His person and to establish an alliance with Him.

All the characteristics of the personality of God show how marvelous and perfect He is and how much He should be admired and reverenced. His love, wisdom, mercy, sovereignty, power, authority, glory, justice, perfection, holiness, forgiveness, kindness, patience, compassion, etc. are attributes that must be acknowledged by His children and many of these attributes mirrored through us, as being generated by Him.

This is according to II Corinthians 3:18:

"But we all, with unveiled face, beholding as in a mirror the glory of the Lord, are being transformed into the same image from glory to glory, just as by the Spirit of the Lord".

The characteristics of God will be manifested in us and through us as his children and we will be transformed into His character; however, we will only be able to reflect them by developing an intimate relationship with and a continuous practice of adoring God.

To adore means "to devote reverence and veneration to a deity in prayer". From the Latin *"adorare"*, which is the combination of "ad" + "orare".

We become similar to whom or what we adore. This is written in Psalms 135: 15 through 18, where the psalmist talks about those who deposit their trust in images of sculpture:

*"The idols of the nations are silver and gold, the work of men's hands. They have mouths, but they speak not, they have eyes, but they see not; they have ears, but they hear not, nor is there any breath in their mouths. Those who make them **will be like them, and so will all who trust in them!**"*.

Trust involves devotion, belief and confidence, it is surrendering oneself to the one or what the person adores. These verses (also mentioned in Psalms 115), reveal something extremely dangerous for those who trust in images of sculpture, because they will become like them. They will die, for only the dead have the characteristics described in the Psalm, that is, having a mouth but not being able to speak, having eyes but not seeing, having ears but not hearing, having feet and not walking and a nose and not smelling.

On the other hand, this also shows something very important and wonderful: that the person who trusts become like the one he deposits trust in. This gives us the glorious and privileged opportunity to receive the personality of God and become like Him through adoration. When we adore Him, we will never be the same again!

It is important for us to understand the differences between praise and worship. Many people think they are the same and end up not reaping the benefits of the glorious experience of adoration.

Praise is the expression of a compliment and acknowledgement of a person to another, but it relates to something performed by such person. It is like praising God for all He has given and done; for salvation, health, family, home, job, sustenance, etc. etc.

This means that praise is due to God for what He has given and done for us, which we will express through words and/or songs that will express our gratitude and our acknowledgment of Him, therefore, Praise is more related to what the **hands** of God have done for us and given to us.

Worship/adoration is more related to acknowledging who God is and, as mentioned above, it requires reverence, devotion and veneration, that is, an intimate surrender and worship that is so real that it does not depend only on words, but can also be expressed through tears, silence, contemplation, admiration, lifting of the hands, prayer in the spirit, etc. Adoration is more related to the **face** of God and who He **is**.

Jesus said, with respect to worship, in John 4:23 and 24:

"But the hour is coming, and now is, that the true worshipers will worship the Father in spirit and truth, for such the Father seeks to worship him. God is Spirit, and it is necessary for those who worship him must worship in spirit and truth".

We can worship God in any place and at any time, but an opportunity for those that do so after entering in the holy of holies (which is evidently a spiritual place), brings another dimension to adoration, which is much more excellent and more intense than any other worship experience that a human being can have, because it is in this place that the Shekinah of God is manifested.

Praise or worship is directly connected to the disposition of the person's heart. The heart has to be grateful for what the Lord has done and given. How can someone worship God from whom he holds an ungrateful or revolted heart? If the person is holding God responsible for all the problems and challenges he/she is facing and even things that have happened in his/her life that he/she doesn't understand and disagree, believing that God isn't good and merciful, then he won't be able to praise or adore God with sincerity.

Recognizing the mercy of God and appreciating even the small things the Lord has done and given is essential for a real expression of praise and worship to be produced.

Cultivate a grateful heart. Recognize the mercy of the Lord upon your life. We all deserve eternal condemnation and death, but He is so loving and merciful that He has sent his only son to die for you and for me, bleeding and suffering in the cross to pay for our salvation and eternal life with Him.

Maintain a grateful heart, even in adversity, according to the amplified translation of I Thessalonians 5:18:

"Thank [God] in everything [no matter what the circumstances may be, be thankful and give thanks], for this is the will of God for you [who are] in Christ Jesus [the Revealer and Mediator of that will]".

Researchers have found that a grateful heart prevents sicknesses and diseases. Psychosomatic diseases are the ones that are originated in the emotions, like: grudge, unforgiveness, hate, wrath, rebellion, etc., and transferred to the body, creating diseases and infirmities.

One of the ways to find out if our hearts are grateful is to check if we are coveting someone else's life or what they have. This is a demonstration that we are not satisfied with what we are and have. Let the Lord search your heart and start developing gratitude and recognizing all the things He has done and given to you. This is one of the most important attitudes to legitimately praise and worship our wonderful savior and Lord.

It is God's desire for each person to know the necessary steps and the preparation needed to enter into the holy of holies and for such person to experience the greatest revelation any one can have in all the history of mankind: the revelation of the person of God and His SHEKINAH.

The preparation we are mentioning is recorded in the book of Hebrews 10:19 through 22:

"Therefore, brethren, having boldness to enter the Holiest by the blood of Jesus, by a new and living way which He consecrated for us, through the veil, that is, His flesh, and having a High Priest over the house of God, let us draw near with a true heart in full assurance of faith, having our hearts sprinkled from an evil conscience and our bodies washed with pure water".

God wants to reveal himself to us, making us like Him and worship is the most effective and pure way for that to happen.

In the next chapters we will explore the details of each one of the steps to enter into this glorious place and experience the SHEKINAH...

CHAPTER 4

1ˢᵗ Requirement to enter the holy of holies:

Boldness

The book of Hebrews teaches us in a practical and objective way the attitudes that we must have to enter into the holy of holies and experience the Shekinah. These attitudes will prepare us to enter therein, just as the high priest had to prepare himself, because the Shekinah is not something trivial or of little value, but rather it is something very strong, valuable, holy and glorious, which must be respected and recognized for what it is.

Hebrews 10:19 says:

"Therefore, brethren, having boldness to enter the Holiest..."

This is the first requirement to enter into the holy of holies.

In the original text, the word used for boldness is *"Parrésia"*, which also means firmness and determination.

Boldness is required because it demonstrates that we truly want to enter therein. It is not for one who is indecisive or afraid to enter. It is for someone who is decided and resolute! This has to do with the motivation that comes from the heart of the individual who truly wishes to enter the presence of God, to acknowledge His attributes and to demonstrate the individual's love for his/her marvelous and true Father.

In yet another translation, the word used is "confidence". Boldness does not mean that the individual is arrogant, naughty, ill-mannered, aggressive or familiar. The impression we often have of someone who is bold is that of an individual who acts in a preposterous manner, without respect, aggressive, but this is not what the word is trying to convey when it refers to boldness. It is directly linked to courage and to how much the individual is really determined and motivated. If the individual is holding on to the past, to what people say about him, what other people think, the temporary difficulties and tribulations he/she is going through, his/her own faults, the accusations the devil is making against him, the repressive upbringing he/she had, the rejections he/she suffered in his/her relationships, the hurts, the negative feelings and thoughts, or even the frustrations suffered for not having achieved or received something from God and is upset with Him, such individual will give up and will not have the determination it takes to enter into the holy of holies.

When we make the decision to enter, we must also be aware that all things that are circumstantial fade out and lose their strength when we enter the holy of holies and witness the SHEKINAH. This does not mean that problems and wounds are of no importance. What we need to understand is that, when we enter into the presence of God, we enter in such great, marvelous and special dimension that all other things are minute, circumstantial and limited in time.

Unfortunately, we are living in a time where things and personal accomplishments are valued to an extreme; so many people think they are the center of everything and everything revolves around them and in their favor. Egocentrism and selfishness have become the norm and altruism and compassion for others, their difficulties and needs have become the exception. In this current mentality, even God is being treated as an assistant, a servant at the disposal of the individual, who must be available and meeting his/her wishes, expectations and desires. Here is where pride is revealed, which is the mistake a person makes with respect to his/her real condition; the person who thinks he/she is the one who has the autonomy, the power, when in reality God is the one who has all the power and we are the ones who are His servants and ought to obey and adore Him.

That is why entering into the holy of holies is so important. In order to enter into it we must humble ourselves, acknowledging that God is the one who has the power and we must recognize the importance of what really matters, that the focus there is not on us, but on God! He is the center of the universe; He is also the center of our lives; we adore Him; we acknowledge who He is, that He is almighty, that He deserves all the glory; we acknowledge His lordship, His majesty and holiness; that from Him, by Him and for Him are all things; that He is worthy to receive all the honor; that he is wonderful, holy, just, loyal, true, good, glorious, magnificent, extraordinary, sovereign, wise, merciful, compassionate, loving, etc., so we end up declaring just as the apostle John declared, "He must increase and I must decrease"! (John 3:30)

In the word of God, we see that one of the most important qualifications God wants to see in us is courage and boldness. A double mind demonstrates insecurity and instability; it is impossible for us to trust someone like that. This is according to James 1:6-8:

"But let him ask in faith, with no doubting, for he who doubts is like a wave of the sea driven and tossed by the wind. For let not that man suppose that he will receive anything from the Lord; he is a double-minded man, unstable in all his ways".

Instability is very harmful, producing only negative fruit, but so are fear and timidity, which are of no value to anyone, mainly a child of God. These were the characteristics of the men who were disqualified and sent back home by God through Gideon, as written in Judges 7:13:

"Now therefore, proclaim in the hearing of the people, saying, 'Whoever is fearful and afraid, let him turn and depart at once from Mount Gilead.'" And twenty-two thousand of the people returned, and ten thousand remained".

We see in this verse that over 2/3 of the warriors went home, due to fear and because they were afraid. In a war it is impossible to trust and depend on fearful and trembling soldiers. God was the one who rejected them. He expects to find in us a conviction, a certainty and a boldness that are required of those who know who He is and there is nothing or no one who can go against Him.

The decision is ours. Either we will be the type that always has one foot on one side and one on the other, not fully on either side, or we will decide to become bold in our faith, resolved and firm to advance, just like Joshua and Caleb, who declared that the giants of the earth were nothing before God and became the only ones of that multitude who entered the land!

God is waiting for you to take a position and the decision you take will make a difference in all areas of your life. You must have courage and boldness to enter into the presence of God and worship Him in spirit and in truth.

There is a word that people don't use very often, which is "RESOLUTE", which means: determined, unwavering, resolved, decided, purposeful. It expresses a mind and heart that got rid of all the negativity and second thoughts and took a position and stand.

Search your heart and get rid of all the fear, doubt and double thoughts and feelings, and take a stand in boldness, courage and resolve and say to yourself:

"I WILL enter the holy of holies to express my love and appreciation to my Lord and savior! Nothing will hinder me to do it! I stand in boldness and courage; this is the will of God, who is seeking true worshippers and He already found one. I AM one of them!

CHAPTER 5

2ⁿᵈ Requirement to enter the holy of holies:

Through the Blood of Jesus

Hebrews 10:19 says, *"...through the blood of Jesus"*

There is great misunderstanding concerning the real power of the blood of Jesus, the forgiveness and the grace of God.

We will not be able to enter into the holy of holies by our own righteousness or good deeds. Only through the blood of Jesus. If it is by our righteousness, that is, for what we have done, conquered, achieved, because we obeyed the word of God, because we gained a soul for Jesus or even because we believe we deserve or are good, we will not give the blood of Jesus the merit and the importance it truly has. All correct and good things that we do are important and God expects us to do them, but it is not what God wants to see when we enter into His presence, but rather the blood of His son.

We should enter into His presence by the merits of Jesus and fully covered by His blood, because only His blood has sufficient power to purify us from all sins, according to I John 1:9:

"If we confess our sins, He is faithful and just to forgive us our sins and to cleanse us from all unrighteousness".

My wife and I, in counseling hundreds of people one on one, were surprised at the number of them who have attended church for years and are not sure of their salvation. They think that because they still have faults God cannot really take them to live with Him in heaven forever. This shows how troubling the matter is, that so many people have no understanding of the real power there is in the blood of Jesus shed on the cross. It is more powerful than the blood of all animals born to date, if they were all sacrificed and their blood shed. The Bible tells us about this in Hebrews 9:13 and 14:

"For if the blood of bulls and goats and the ashes of a heifer, sprinkling the unclean, sanctifies for the purifying of the flesh, how much more shall the blood of Christ, who through the eternal Spirit offered Himself without spot to God, cleanse your conscience from dead works to serve the living God?"

And what is recorded in Isaiah 1:18:

"Come now, and let us reason together", Says the Lord "Though your sins are like scarlet, they shall be as white as snow; though they are red like crimson, they shall be as wool".

This gives us the boldness, determination and fearlessness to enter, because we do not have to worry about sins or mistakes or the idea that God only accepts us if we appear with some kind of works, our own righteousness or by the good deeds and conquests we have achieved.

Therefore, neither our sins hinder us, nor our good deeds enable us to enter into the holy of holies.

In order for us to have a clearer idea of the power there is in the blood of Jesus, it is interesting to note the process God uses so that the blood of Jesus has the power to redeem us:

When we read in Genesis 3:15, God said this to the serpent:

"And I will put enmity between you and the woman, and between your offspring and hers; he will crush your head, and you will strike His heel".

In this prophetic word, the Lord was foretelling the most important process for the blood of Jesus to be effective and work in our lives to purify us.

The antivenom serum is produced with the venom from the serpent. This venom is injected in horses, which will produce antibodies for this toxin. Blood is drawn from the horse to separate the antibodies in order to produce the serum.

This explains why it was necessary for Jesus to be wounded. It was by receiving the venom of the serpent (our sin) Himself that he produced the antibodies and the antigen so that today anyone who receives His blood can be totally purified and cured from this venom called sin.

Glory be to God for the extremely painful sacrifice Jesus suffered on the cross for us! It was the shedding of His blood that paid the price of our redemption, according to Revelation 5:9:

"And they sang a new song, saying: "You are worthy to take the scroll, and to open its seals; for You were slain, and have redeemed us to God by Your blood out of every tribe and tongue and people and nation".

We must believe in the blood of Jesus and in the power it has to purify from all sin. Visualize all your sins being washed away, confessing and repenting from each one of them. God loves you and wants this powerful and redeeming work that His Son has done on the cross to become reality in your life! There is no more sin or accusation that weighs against you, if you are purified by the blood of Jesus; believe in this unchanging and eternal truth!

CHAPTER 6

3rd requirement to enter the holy of holies:

By The New And Living Way

Hebrews 10:20 and 21:

"...by a new and living way which He consecrated for us, through the veil, that is, His flesh, and having a High Priest over the house of God..."

This way was not opened before, but it was opened when Jesus died on the cross as it is written in Matthew 27: 50 and 51:

"And Jesus cried out again with a loud voice, and yielded up His spirit. Then, behold, the veil of the temple was torn in two from top to bottom; and the earth quaked, and the rocks were split".

When Jesus was chastised and whipped, His flesh was literally opened by the ends of the whips. According to historians, Jesus received 39 whippings on his body, where the nails on the ends of the whips penetrated His flesh and, when the soldiers pulled them, His flesh was lifted, exposing muscles and other internal parts of His body. This had been predicted by the prophet Isaiah in chapter 53, verse 5:

> *"But He was wounded for our transgressions, He was bruised for our iniquities; the chastisement for our peace was upon Him, and by His stripes we are healed".*

This "bruising" was necessary so that He could receive in His own body all of our curses, accusations and sins, so that we could finally attain the peace <u>of</u> God and the peace <u>with</u> God.

Now, we must put this into practice in our lives. It is by the new and living way that we must understand the difference between a door and a way; a door is an event, that is, a single fact that defines between "inside" and "outside". However, the way means a process, that is, something that has a "beginning", a "middle" and leads to a place somewhere, that is, an "end". The way is something that shows a chronological order of facts.

Another important point is that the way is living, that is, it is dynamic and comprehensive. From the time we start taking steps in the new way, we begin to perceive that it is a living way, because we will identify that not only all the plagues and curses on humanity were embedded in the flesh of Jesus, but we will also be able to identify each of our own plagues and curses which must be transferred to it, that is, we no longer need to carry anything that had already been carried by Jesus, the same way there is no law that requires someone to pay twice for the same crime. If He has already paid the price, we no longer need to pay it again; if He has already carried it, we do not need to carry it again.

By this new way, we will be able to destroy by faith all curses that sin has brought into our lives.

In order for this to be put into practice, place your faith in action and declare that all curses that disobedience, sin and rebellion have brought into your life are now placed on the flesh of Jesus. See with the eyes of faith all of your iniquities, miseries, illnesses, mistakes, wrong desires, perversions, compulsions, anguish, defeats, accusations, emotional sickness, rejections, works of darkness, mental illnesses, pains, bitterness, depression, negative arguments, lusts, works of the flesh, witchcraft, disturbances, oppressions, destruction, robbery and death embedded in the flesh of Jesus.

It is also then that you must look deep into your heart to see if there is someone who has wronged you and that you have not yet forgiven and decide to forgive this person completely.

If you have not done this yet, Jesus taught us that if we do not forgive, the Father will not forgive us either (see Mark 11:26). Jesus also speaks about this in the prayer He taught in Matthew 6:12:

"...and forgive us our debts, as we forgive our debtors".

This means that when we pray this prayer, we are saying to God, "Lord, please, do You see how I am forgiving individuals who did me wrong, treated me badly, spoke ill of me, lied about, offended and betrayed me? I ask that you forgive me exactly in this same manner and measure!"

It is also very important not to reminisce and relive matters that have already been resolved, that is, if each point and matter in the past that had to be dealt with has already been opened, confessed, cured and treated by the Lord Jesus, we cannot keep reliving and acting as if the sacrifice and all the suffering Jesus endured had not been valid. The past is one of the things the devil uses the most in the lives of individuals, because he cannot accuse the future which has not happened yet and cannot accuse the present because it is still happening, but he accuses the past because he knows that we do not have the power to go back in time and change what was done.

Therefore, we need to forget *"those things left behind"*, as Paul teaches in Philippians 3:13 and 14:

"Brethren, I do not count myself to have apprehended; but one thing I do, forgetting those things which are behind and reaching forward to those things which are ahead, I press toward the goal for the prize of the upward call of God in Christ Jesus".

Forgetting our sins does not mean that we lose our memory, but rather that they do not remain as something latent, something that keeps on tormenting us; but, if somehow we remember something that happened, we remember it without shame, vexation, bitterness, weight or condemnation.

In Jeremiah 31:34B, the Bible tells us that God forgets our sins:

"....For I will forgive their iniquity, and their sin I will remember no more".

If we do not leave our past behind, we will be as if trying to walk backwards with a heavy rock tied to our leg. If we do not interrupt this process from being a part of our lives, what starts as sadness will become disappointment and disappointment will become depression and depression will become bitterness and it will contaminate everyone around us, according to Hebrews 12:15:

"See to it that no one fail to obtain the grace of God; that no "root of bitterness" spring up and cause trouble, and by this many become defiled".

Keep in mind that the believer shall live by faith, meaning that it requires action from our part. Verse 21 declares that we have a great priest over the house of God. This great priest is Jesus, according to Hebrews 9:12 through 14:

*"Not with the blood of goats and calves, but with His own blood He entered the Most Holy Place once for all, having obtained eternal redemption. For if the blood of bulls and goats and the ashes of a heifer, sprinkling the unclean, sanctifies for the purifying of the flesh, **how much more** shall the blood of Christ, who through the eternal Spirit offered Himself without spot to God, cleanse your conscience from dead works to serve the living God?"*

Jesus presented Himself before God in the holy of holies, something that only the high priest could do, that is, show that He is this great priest mentioned in verse 21. But He did not enter with the blood of animals, but with His own blood, making this type of sacrifice eternally sufficient before God and never again would it be necessary to have sacrifices with the shedding of animal blood for the purification and the atonement of sins. GLORY TO GOD FOR THE BLOOD OF JESUS; an immaculate and uncontaminated blood, the only one capable of purifying us from our sins, as well as our conscience from dead works, attitudes, sins and disobedience we commit which now, by the love, grace and mercy of God, are forever embedded in the flesh of Jesus!

In the Old Testament, only those of the tribe of Levi were separated for the priesthood ministry, according to God's commandment in Exodus 28. After Jesus died, each person has the responsibility to present him/herself before God with the blood of the sacrifice made by Him on the cross. This responsibility is no longer delegated to someone special. This is made clear in the book of I Peter 2:9:

"But you are the chosen generation, a <u>royal priesthood</u>, a holy nation, God's own people, that you may declare the wonderful deeds of him who called you out of darkness into his marvelous light";

Also in Revelation 1:6:

"And made us a kingdom, <u>priests to his God and Father</u>, to him be the glory and dominion for ever and ever. Amen".

Still in Revelation 5:10:

"And has made them a kingdom and <u>priests</u> to our God, and they shall reign on earth".

Our priesthood authority granted by God can't be questioned or challenged by men. The authority the Lord has given to us is extraordinary, something that enables us to enter into the Holy of holies with confidence and doesn't depend on the educational degrees, years of experience as Christians or even our personal achievements.

This new and living way, which is the flesh of Jesus, already took all the sins and curses, so now we can see this happening in our own lives through the eyes of faith and, after achieving the other side, be joyous and rejoicing for the freedom and victory we've accomplished, enjoying the wonderful promise registered in I Peter 2:24:

"Who his own self bare our sins in his own body on the tree, that we, being dead to sins, should live unto righteousness: by whose stripes you were healed."

Now, that you already have the boldness and the blood of Jesus has cleansed you, it is time for you to take the third step to enter into the most holy place: leave in the flesh of Jesus all that is hurting your body and emotions and take possession of the peace that surpasses all understanding and let it take over and control you, so you end up the "living way" totally different than when you started.

CHAPTER 7

4th Requirement to enter the holy of holies:

A True Heart

Hebrews 10:22: *"draw near with a true heart"*...

A true heart is the heart which doesn't have hidden intentions. We do not enter into the holy of holies because we have any motivation other than to worship God. I do not mean to say that God is not interested in our problems and needs. But we must understand that worship is not something to be used as a form of barter with God. We do not enter into His presence to collect from him or with the intention of receiving some kind of extra favor because we are doing something the majority isn't. God is the one who is giving us the opportunity to acknowledge who He is and his attributes and by worshiping, be conformed to Him.

That is why Jesus talked about the Father seeking someone to worship him in spirit and in truth. In truth means that which is pure in its motivation. This is not the time to ask, but rather to give thanks and honor God. Proverbs 20:5 says:

"The purposes of a person's heart are like deep waters, but one who has insight draws them out".

The real purpose is that which is in the deep of the heart and is what, in the end of the day, will be done. Jesus declared that it is from the heart that come the intentions that become actions.

Therefore, the true heart is the heart that is totally motivated to simply enter into the presence of God and worship Him, in spite of circumstances, emotions, thoughts or any other influence, acknowledging the privilege that is to be able to be in the presence of the creator of all the universe, the greatest, most admirable and most glorious being that ever was or will be.

As we discussed earlier, our soul has a strong tendency to worry and be anxious, pressured by both personal and general problems, circumstances and interests. This creates a motivation for us to seek God with the intention that He will solve our problems, our frustrations and help us to achieve what we purpose, which ends up becoming a vicious cycle: problems, frustrations and desires pressure the soul, creating anxiety and worry, which leads to prayers and petitions for relief. And the cycle repeats itself. Prayers become a routine for almost only requests and more requests.

Can you imagine if the relationship between a father and son would always be like this? The son would only approach the father at the time of need, to ask for a bunch of things, not interested in hearing what the father has to say, not acknowledging everything that has already been done by the father, not hugging the father, not telling him that he/she loves him, not showing gratitude for what the father has done for him/her and goes away only to come back later with more requests.

Many times we end up thinking that we are the center of everything and that God is our helper, or even a servant who will give us and do whatever we need and desire for Him to do. Lets see: how many of us say a prayer like this: "God, I want you to do this and that, bless such thing, such person, and also do this and that to them, do not allow for such a thing to happen, protect such a person, protect so and so, etc., etc..." Does it not give the impression of someone giving orders to a servant? This does not mean we should not ask, but many of us have had a mistaken attitude and developed a relationship with God as if He were Santa Claus. Instead, we must place ourselves at God's disposal, willing to obey Him, being thankful for all that He has done, humble ourselves before His Majesty and <u>also</u> ask for what we need. Examine your heart. If deep down you and your life are still more important than God, you are practicing selfishness and you need to come down from the throne of your heart and be a true worshiper, that is, place God first in your life, making Him your Lord and King, having Him seat on the throne of your heart.

The priorities must be correctly established in our hearts. Because of this, there is a great danger which was mentioned by the apostle Paul in Philippians 3:18 and 19

"For many walk, of whom I have told you often, and now tell you even weeping, that they are the enemies of the cross of Christ: whose end is destruction, whose god is their belly, and whose glory is in their shame - <u>who set their mind on earthly things</u>".

True worshipers not only acknowledge the need of the cross, but also decline to be egotistical, that is, idolaters of themselves and surrender themselves fully to the lordship of Jesus Christ, who is not only their savior, but also their Lord, commanding all aspects and areas of their lives.

We must examine our relationship with our beloved Father and develop an intimacy with Him that will make us walk in the light, dwell in His shelter and rest under His wings, according to Psalm 91:1, where our emotions, thoughts and desires are controlled and submitted to Him and where we find rest for our souls.

Jesus offers you resting now. Stop all anxiety and worry that have never helped anything or resolved any of the problems and difficulties you have faced thus far; on the contrary, they have compelled you to make decisions under stress, at the risk of creating even more problems.

The invitation from Jesus stands firm to this date, according to Matthew *11:28-30:*

"Come to me, all who labor and are heavy laden, and I will give you rest. Take my yoke upon you and learn from me; for I am gentle and lowly in heart, and you will find rest for your souls. For my yoke is easy, and my burden is light".

The true heart is ready to enter into the holy of holies because it has submitted its anxieties, worries, desires, dreams, wants and wishes to the Lordship of Jesus and has only one desire: to offer Him the pure and legitimate adoration of a sincere heart.

The true heart is also the one that has deposited its trust and total surrender to the Lord and His will. It will say, with total openness and sincerity, just like Jesus said in Luke 22:42: "Not my will, but thy will be done".

When our heart isn't true, we just can't accomplish much, because God can't be fooled; He knows everything and even our hearts; nothing is covered or hidden from him.

If your heart isn't true, repent and confess this sin and receive the wonderful forgiveness and the peace that comes with it and you will have achieved the fourth step to enter into the most holy place and experience the wonderful Shekinah...

CHAPTER 8

5th Requirement to enter the holy of holies:

Full Assurance of Faith

Hebrews 10:22 ...*in full assurance of faith*...

In Hebrews 11:1, the Bible tells us that faith:

"....is the assurance of things hoped for, the conviction of things not seen".

Faith is neither a feeling nor a positive thought. It will, of course, affect our thoughts and feelings, but it must not be negatively influenced by them. Faith is the clear and real assurance of something that is the will of God. The faith assigned by God to each one, in accordance with Romans 12:3b,

"...but to think soberly, as God has assigned to each one a measure of faith.".

Faith is not a privilege of a group of individuals or religion. It was given by God for all, in different measures, according to this verse above.

The secret is not in having faith, but rather where we direct it. Even the atheist has faith: he BELIEVES that God does not exist.

Many Indians direct their faith to the sun, the moon, nature. Some direct their faith to a rabbit's foot, others to sculptured images, others to a religion or even a church or denomination or a great preacher.

When Jesus said in Mark 11:22: "And Jesus answered them, "Have faith in God", he was giving the correct direction for our faith: in God.

Faith is something so important to us that the Bible teaches in Hebrews 6:26 that the righteous will <u>live</u> by faith. This means that faith is our spiritual oxygen and not an occasional accessory that we wear once in a while or something we only use in the time of need, when we face difficulties.

The importance of faith is so impressive that even Jesus, with all of his power, was limited in the operation of this power based on the faith of each one. In Matthew 13:58:

"And he did not do many mighty works there, because of their unbelief".

He certainly had all the power to perform such miracles, but he was limited by their faith, which was inoperative. In reality, unbelief is faith used negatively, that is, I believe it is not going to happen! I believe everything will go wrong! I believe all is going downhill! This is unbelief; it means to use faith in opposition to the will of God.

If we examine the gospels, Jesus said on many occasions, "be it done according to your faith"! He never said, "be it done according to my power or my strength". There was a man who said, "help me in my small faith..." I would like to ask: if Jesus was to approach you now and ask: "what would you like for me to do for you?" and after you answered he would say, "ok, let it be done according to your faith", what would happen? Would you be receiving what you need? Or would you prefer to keep on asking for it over and over, thinking that if you ask every day for a long time, God will end up being convinced that you really need it and will grant your request?

James 1:6 through 8, says:

"But let him ask in faith, with no doubting, for he who doubts is like a wave of the sea driven and tossed by the wind. For let not that man suppose that he will receive anything from the Lord; he is a double-minded man, unstable in all his ways".

This means that, without faith, I could ask 1 million times and not receive anything!

Once Jesus said, "Fear not, only believe!" This demonstrates that emotions or thoughts will try our faith, but we must only believe. Pure faith is what leads us to victory. Just like Jesus said in Mark 11:24

"Truly I say to you, whoever says to this mountain, "Be taken up and cast into the sea, and does not doubt in his heart, but believes that what he says will come to pass, it will be done for him".

This means that the word is the result of faith, that is, as it is written, "I believed, and so I spoke" II Corinthians 4:13 – who truly believes, expresses with words. The woman with the issue of blood did this. It is written that she said,

"...If I only touch his garment, I will be made well". (Matthew 9:21)

Doubt or unbelief will only hinder and block the entrance to the holy of holies. Throw away all doubt and believe, for it is written in Hebrews 11:6:

"Without faith it is impossible to please God. For whoever would draw near to God must believe that he exists and that he rewards those who seek him".

A few years ago, God opened my mind concerning an aspect of faith I had never noticed before: faith is like a grain of a seed, and as such it goes through the same process of germination as the seed. This gave me a clear vision of why my faith was not producing fruit and needed a change of attitude in order for it to produce. Let me share with you this understanding:

In Matthew 17:20, Jesus said:

"He replied, "Because you have so little faith. Truly I tell you, if you have faith as small as mustard seed, you can say to this mountain, "Move from here to there" and it will move. Nothing will be impossible for you".

Definition of seed: something that carries within itself all the characteristics of what created it and the power to reproduce it.

The grain of seed consists of three elements: core/embryo, shell/ seed coat and cotyledon/endosperm.

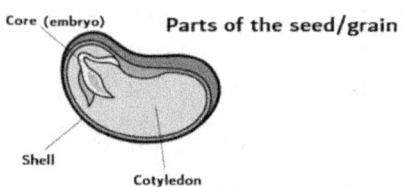

All of the genetic substance is lodged in the core, which must be released in order for the multiplying property of the seed to be placed in action.

Jesus said, in *John 12:24*:

"truly, truly, I say to you, unless a grain of wheat falls into the earth and dies, it remains alone; but if it dies, it bears much fruit".

In this verse, Jesus was speaking about another grain representing himself, that is, that he would have to die, but since He consisted of spirit, soul and body, just like the grain consists of three parts, what died on the cross was neither the spirit nor the soul, but rather the body, that is, just like the seed, the shell, the outer part, the housing is what died.

Therefore, what is part of the shell must be broken (like what many of us experienced watching in the school, when we placed a bean on the top of a wet piece of cotton and watched it sprout).

It is the shell that hinders the core from being released and producing. Like Jesus, if His body had not died, His spirit and His soul would not have been released. So it is with faith. The "shell" must die for the core to be released. Some of the characteristics of the shell are listed below, but there may be others. Identify in your life wether the shell is hindering your faith from producing the works it is supposed to produce.

The following are some of the characteristics of the shell of the faith/grain:

1) OPPOSING ARGUMENTS (reasoning): the mind tries to "understand" or "rationalize" what faith is trying to produce; the mind dominates, does not accept, does not submit to simply receiving something that it cannot control or understand. The imagination blocks faith, arguing with itself saying: "how is this supposed to happen"? "This makes no sense, it is very complicated, this is impossible to happen"...

Here are some practical examples of thoughts that "attack" our faith: a doctor gives a certain diagnosis and that nothing can change it; the bank manager says there is nothing that can be done financially for your case; the spouse says there is no more hope for the marriage; someone in church say they no longer wish to serve God or come to this church; the son is rebellious; the interviewer says there is no way he can hire for the job, etc. etc. Since the mind is limited, it does not conceive how this can be reversed and ends up blocking faith. That is why the Bible teaches us in Psalms 94:11:

"The Lord knows the thoughts of man, that they are futile".

Also, Mark 10:27 says:

"But Jesus looked at them and said, "With man it is impossible, but not with God; for with God all things are possible."

You have to break the shell of the seed of faith of the negative thought and opposing reasoning by believing the supernatural is going to happen, even knowing that it doesn't make sense, nor fit in your mind.

2) UNBELIEF (opposing faith) is to believe that what is wished for will not happen, or to believe that the negative, the bad will happen, in opposition to what is desired, or what the bible says about

it. For example: It means to see a spot on the skin and immediately believe it is cancer; or that everything will go wrong in life; that the promotion or raise is not going to happen; that people will abandon you; that money will be short; it means to direct faith to what is opposing of what it should be producing, which is good and not evil, a blessing and not a curse.

To use something so powerful and wonderful given by God such as faith, and, instead of producing positive things, make it to produce negative things is one of the greatest attitudes of disrespect to God and to what He has promised; it is to agree with the devil that God is not good, that He does not desire what is good for us and that what the Bible teaches in Jeremiah 29:11 is not true:

"For I know the plans I have for you, says the Lord, plans for welfare and not for evil, to give you a future and a hope".

Unbelief blocks the operation of signs and miracles of God, according to Matthew 13:58:

"Now he did not do many mighty works there because of their unbelief".

In spite of the fact that Jesus had all the power to perform wonderful things and produce extraordinary signs, He was limited because of their unbelief, for they believed much more in the Jesus they saw growing up in that city than in the Jesus who was now before their eyes with all the power to perform miracles in their lives.

You have to break the shell of faith of unbelief, if you have it, by turning the negative into positive, evil towards good. God is good and you have to believe He is.

3) BAD EXAMPLES (bad news) means to base faith on the experience of others based on examples that "did not work out"; it is when an individual, who has witnessed great and supernatural miracles that God performed many, many times, values more that, which did not happen or that which such individual heard somehow it did not work out or did not happen in the way the individual expected. The frustrated individual went out spreading that faith does not work and that prayer and belief were of no avail. This

also happens more often in churches that present a "supermarket" type of God, who is at the service of people, a place where they go, choose what they want and then leave. They place plans and desires in their minds, many times motivated by the desires and lusts of the flesh and want God to be "blessing" them, that is, they want God to do or give what they want, in the form and time they expect Him to.

This behavior is very dangerous and places the person who thinks like this in a very slippery terrain, creating great risks for disappointments and frustrations, because they don't receive everything they desire. The problem is that this kind of behavior from an individual, spreads out bad news and distort the reality of how the true faith works. If we keep on listening to someone like this, we are going to be frustrated and think faith doesn't work.

You must protect your ears by filtering what you hear by the word of God. Also, one of the best ways to be protected from bad news is to avoid contact with negative people; those that only talk and focus in negative and destructive talking.

If the negative news and information is keeping you from believing, you have to break that shell of the seed of faith now, confessing the word of God regarding the miracle or need you have.

4) DOUBTS (is what I am desiring and asking the will of God?) The Bible declares what the will of God is with respect to the various situations in life. Ignorance to what the Bible declares concerning a certain matter creates doubts as to whether or not that is the will of God. That is why people are afraid that what they need cannot be achieved or accomplished, and therefore their faith is not put into action, that is, instead of being assured of the things they hope for, it becomes an uncertainty and people do not receive the blessing. Examples:

- Would it be the will of God to heal? Of course, according to I Peter 2:24;
- Would it be the will of God to supply my needs? Of course, according to Philippians 4:19;

- Would it be the will of God to save my family? Of course, according to Acts 16:31;
- Would it be the will of God for me to feel joy? Of course, according to Philippians 4:4.
- Would it be the will of God for me to be forgiven of my sins? Of course, according to I John 1:9 and Isaiah 1:18.

See what the Word says in I John 5:14 in order for us to receive God's blessings:

"And this is the confidence that we have in him, that if we ask anything <u>according to his will</u> he hears us".

God is pleased when one of his children comes before Him mentioning his Word, not demanding or in a petulant manner, but believing in what he promised. He will provide what is being sought, for he fulfills his Word, according to Jeremiah 1:12:

"Then the Lord said to me, "I am watching over my word to perform it".

If you don't know if what you need is the will of God, search His word, look for the blessings Jesus conquered for you and break the shell of uncertainty if that is the will of God or not.

5) FEELINGS AND EMOTIONS (roller coaster). In Mark 9:23, the Bible does not say that all things are possible to those who feel, but rather to those who believe. In Jeremiah 17:9, the Bible declares something strong:

"The heart is deceitful above all things, and desperately corrupt; who can know it"?

Emotions and feelings are part of the soul (mind and emotions) and the soul is like a roller coaster, sometimes it is at the top, assured, enthusiastic, excited and believing; sometimes it is at the bottom, in despair, frustration and unbelief.

How many times I've encountered people saying: "I am not feeling I will be healed", or: "I am not feeling the Lord is going to provide for my rent this month", or even: "I don't feel God really loves me". This is the biggest deceit…believing in ones own feeling and emotions, instead in what God promises in His word. What is even more interesting is the volatility the heart has: believing, assured and trusting one minute and, after a negative phone call or text from someone, goes all the way to the other side doubting, frustrated and not believing the next minute.

It is one of the greatest challenges we face: believing in what God has promised, even if our feelings and emotions are trying to make us doubt. Faith must overcome negative emotions and feelings in order for us to attain peace and the assurance that what God has promised He will fulfill.

Jesus said in Mark 11:23:

"For assuredly, I say to you, whoever says to this mountain, 'Be removed and be cast into the sea,' and does not doubt in his heart, but believes that those things he says will be done, he will have whatever he says."

In this verse, Jesus is emphasizing that the heart cannot be doubting and the mouth has to be saying what the heart is believing, which means that it cannot be a contradiction between them, that a consistency and oneness has to be clear, where the mouth is declaring what the heart is believing and the blessing will be accomplished!

If you are feeling that what you need you are not going to receive or the miracle you need isn't going to happen, you must break this shell of the seed of faith and substitute the negative feeling to faith, even against the negative felling or emotion you are having about it.

6) SIZE OF THE PROBLEM (mountain). Many times we tend to believe more readily in smaller situations than in big challenges. When Jesus mentioned the size of the obstacle, He spoke of a mountain, not anything smaller, as is recorded in Matthew 17:20:

"So Jesus said to them, "Because of your unbelief; for assuredly, I say to you, if you have faith as a mustard seed, you will say to this mountain, 'Move from here to there,' and it will move; and nothing will be impossible for you.".

Compared to us, a mountain is something enormous. We don't have the capacity to remove it by ourselves. What Jesus is illustrating is that we will face situations in our lives that are like true mountains, irremovable to our human eyes, but perfectly capable of being removed by the Lord, for what He declares in Isaiah 43:13 is this:

"Indeed before the day was, I am He; And there is no one who can deliver out of My hand; when I act, who can reverse it"?

Examples of the size of the problem:

- Believe for the cure of a headache vs. believe for the cure of a cancer;
- Believe in the miracle for $1,000.00 vs. believe in the miracle for $100,000.00;
- Believe in the solution of little marital discords, vs. believe in the restoration of a marriage, even after the divorce has been signed and the couple have been apart from each other.

Due to the fact that the mountain is much bigger than us, we have the tendency to think it is too big to be removed. Of course, the miracle we need is very big or the problem we are facing is very complicated to be resolved, but our focus must be placed in the power of God, which is much stronger and bigger that any mountain or situation we face or miracle we need.

If this is your case, break this shell of the seed of faith and start believing in God and His might and power to move the mountain and give the miracle you need and resolve the situation you are facing.

8) ATTENTION AND FOCUS ON THE PROBLEM (re-directing attention to where it should be). In Romans 4:19 through 21 we read the following about Abraham:

"And not being weak in faith, he did not consider his own body, already dead (since he was about a hundred years old), and the deadness of Sarah's

womb. He did not waver at the promise of God through unbelief, but he was strengthened in faith, giving glory to God, and being fully convinced that what He had promised He was also able to perform".

When we focus our attention on the problem, we are showing that the problem is more important than God, who has promised us victory.

Abraham could have pitied himself and murmured against God and what He had promised for 25 years, but he opted to simply believe. I believe that at night he would go out and gaze at the stars in the sky, rejoicing and praising God for the families on earth that would be blessed through him, according to what God has promised.

If we focus on the problem, it seems as if that is all we can see before us. Have you ever encountered the type of individual that seems to have nothing else to talk about except his/her problem? You meet this type of individual Sunday morning and as soon as they greet you they begin to talk about the problem that afflicts them. Afterwards or even another day, you run into them again and once again they mention the problem. This shows a behavioral habit that leads the individual to give importance to the problem and to doubt God, who had already promised the victory. This only weakens faith.

Several times, I have observed individuals who, shortly after laying down their problems at the altar, believing that God will resolve them, do see their problems resolved. It is like what I've heard sometimes about a woman who wants to conceive and that is all she talks about every time she meets someone, but then decides to no longer focus on her problem but to put her trust in God, stops talking about it and soon after she conceives!

If this is your situation, you have to break this shell of the seed of faith by re-directing your attention away from the problem and to the One that had promised the miracle to happen.

9) FEAR (overcome by this feeling). Fear is the opposite of faith. The same way water does not mix with oil, no matter how much you try to mix them. That is why Jesus said, in Mark 5:36:

"But ignoring what they said, Jesus said to the ruler of the Synagogue, "Do not fear, only believe".

Fear is a strong aversion to the pain a disappointment, rejection or frustration can create. Just thinking about what an individual can feel because of a disappointment, that individual gives up believing, preferring to lose the blessing rather than "risking" believing and running the risk of being disappointed.

An interesting example of this is found in Psalms 107: 23 through 30:

"Those who go down to the sea in ships, who do business on great waters, they see the works of the Lord, and His wonders in the deep. For He commands and raises the stormy wind, which lifts up the waves of the sea. They mount up to the heavens, they go down again to the depths; Their soul melts because of trouble. They reel to and fro, and stagger like a drunken man, and are at their wits' end. Then they cry out to the Lord in their trouble, And He brings them out of their distresses. He calms the storm, so that its waves are still. Then they are glad because they are quiet; so, He guides them to their desired port"

This passage illustrates very well how faith leads us to "see the works of the Lord, and His wonders in the deep". First, we must overcome fear and decide to navigate, untying our boat from the dock, which represents our comfort zone, our safe haven. In the beginning, all seems normal and we are enthusiastic about reaching our goal. Then God sends the winds and adversities our way, like waves that mount up to heaven, where we are encouraged and we can see everything from above, thinking that we are at the top and exalted by God, when suddenly we find ourselves at the very bottom of the pit, discouraged and regretting having left our comfort zone and we start to miss it. All of this serves to break the structure of independence, pride and self-exaltation of our flesh. That is when, after clearly seeing our fragility, our anguish for not being able to resolve the problem, that we cry out to God asking Him to help us. And it is then that He takes us to the safe port where we desire to be.

I Corinthians 1:29 shows that God does not accept boasting of the flesh, because it is deceitful:

"That no flesh should glory in His presence".

Necessity is the greatest motivator there is. To desire something is very different than to need something. Necessity creates in us a strong tenacity and motivation to obtain what we need, facing challenges, barriers and oppositions that present themselves before us.

Even if in the midst of the storm the thought of returning to our comfort zone comes to our mind, we do not accept it and we continue on.

Fear has to be broken. Only faith can lead us to conquests, victories and accomplishments.

The shell of the seed of faith has to be broken in the area of fear. It is a bold and courageous decision. It is when you take a stand and say: - "Enough is enough, I am living in fear for to long, missing the best God has for me! From now on I will believe what God states in His word and declare it for my life"

10) PASSIVITY (no reaction) – convinced by circumstances. Conformity to circumstances is one of the most frequent reasons why individuals do not move forward and end up not seeing the fulfillment of the promises of God in their lives. These are the people who say, "that's the way it is, nothing changes, I was born this way, my father was this way, my grandfather was this way, and I am destined to be this way, too. The opposite of this happened with Bartimaeus, in the book of Mark 10:47,48:

"And when he heard that it was Jesus of Nazareth, he began to cry out and say, "Jesus, Son of David, have mercy on me!" Then many warned him to be quiet; but he cried out all the more, "Son of David, have mercy on me!""

He was not deterred by those who rebuked him and told him to be silent, but rather he cried out all the more until he received the miracle. Obviously, those who told him to be quiet were not blind, because if they were, they would cry out as much or more than he did.

Passive individuals seek the greater number of excuses and justifications possible so as not to advance and to explain to their own conscience the reason why they do not move forward and do not receive the promises of God. Mediocrity is its greatest characteristic. This type of individual "feeds" his own conscience on the defeat of others, enjoying hearing stories about weaknesses and failures, seeking to appease his own conscience in the event someone asks for the reason for such great laziness and ostracism on their lives.

Some of these people believe in "karma", that is, that their fate is that way and nothing will help change that picture. Others believe in the absurdity of paying the debt of sins and mistakes committed in some past life and that this has to be paid, when the bible doesn't endorse re-incarnation, according to Hebrews 9:27:

"Just as people are destined to die once, and after that to face judgment"

If passivity is your problem, you need to understand that faith is active, not something that makes things and miracles just happen by themselves, but it requires an action on our part, so break this shell of the seed of faith and do what the bible tells us in Ephesians 5:14:

"This is why it is said: "Wake up, sleeper, rise from the dead, and Christ will shine on you."

11) LACK OF PERSISTENCE AND PERSEVERANCE (strengthening, instead of fainting). Faith is like a muscle and needs to be exercised in order to develop. If we do not put faith in practice, it shrinks and dies. Many times the miracle does not happen immediately; it requires persistence and perseverance. Abraham persisted in faith for 25 years until he received the blessing.

Jesus told a parable that demonstrates this very clearly, in Luke 11: 5 through 9:

*"And He said to them, "Which of you shall have a friend, and go to him at midnight and say to him, 'Friend, lend me three loaves; for a friend of mine has come to me on his journey, and I have nothing to set before him'; and he will answer from within and say, 'Do not trouble me; the door is now shut, and my children are with me in bed; I cannot rise and give to you'? I say to you, though he will not rise and give to him because he is his friend, yet because of his **persistence** he will rise and give him as many as he needs. "So I say to you, ask, and it will be given to you; seek, and you will find; knock, and it will be opened to you. For everyone who asks receives, and he who seeks finds, and to him who knocks it will be opened".*

It was because of the persistence of the person that was asking, that his friend stood up and helped him.

At the end of this passage, Jesus mentions 3 types of attitude: ask, seek and knock. These are attitudes that define how determined and persistent we are. If we only ask, we limit our faith. The following step is another attitude: seek. If we still ask and do not receive, we seek. If we seek and do not find, we knock, so that the blessing is received. These 3 attitudes will create the "muscle" of our faith.

It is interesting to see how much people persist and persevere, depending on the situation and the motivation. The majority take up hard orders and commands from their bosses and persist and persevere because they are motivated by the money they depend on to survive and maybe the career they are building up. Others persevere in calling someone they fell in love with, send messages, buy gifts, do everything to conquer that person's heart, motivated by the passion they are feeling.

The problem is that, some others hear a preacher preaching on Sunday and want their miracle or answer to their prayers on Monday morning. If it doesn't happen, they just give up believing and do not persist and persevere, believing what they need will come.

We are the generation of fast food, smart phones and microwaves and don't have the patience older generations had. They had to work hard to prepare and cook their food, send letters or telegrams which took a long time to be answered. We want things to happen immediately or we give up believing.

Perseverance and patience are keys to accomplish the blessings God has for your life. You have to break the shell of the seed of faith in the area of immediate expectations and keep on believing with patience!

12) BAD CONSCIENCE (own justice vs. God's justice) – I John 3:20 through 22:

"know that, if our heart condemns us, greater is God than our heart, and He knows all things. Beloved, if our heart does not condemn us, we trust in God, and anything we ask of Him, we will receive, because we keep His commandments and we do what is pleasing in His sight."

The person that keeps a condemning attitude, won't believe that will receive anything from the Lord, because the conscience will keep on saying that he/she doesn't deserve God's favor, because of sin and guilt.

If we don't believe in the forgiveness of the Lord, we are denying the power of the blood of Jesus, not believing in what the bible declares in I John 1:9:

"If we confess our sins, He is faithful and just to forgive us our sins and to cleanse us from all unrighteousness."

God's justice isn't like ours. We think that, if we fail once or twice, or even after having promised we would never sin again and commit it, we are not worthy of God's forgiveness. Underestimating God's grace is throwing away the price Jesus paid in the cross for our sins. His grace isn't a permit to sin, but it extends to us the undeserved favor of forgiveness and freedom from guilt and condemnation.

Even if we have terrible sins, like Saul, who consented in the murder of Christians, the blood of Jesus is sufficient to cleanse us from all shame and guilt.

Even in the old testament, the Lord promises forgiveness, independent of how dark the sins were, according to Isaiah 1:18:

"Come now, let us reason together," says the LORD. "Though your sins are like scarlet, they will be as white as snow; though they are as red as crimson, they will become like wool."

Take a second look in verses 21 and 22 of 1 John chapter 3. It shows that, if our heart doesn't condemn us, we trust in God, which means that we believe and we will receive anything we ask of him.

If you are not forgiving yourself or not believing the forgiveness God is willing to grant to you, break this shell of the seed of faith now and take control of your own feelings, believing in the promises of God, stating that He forgives the sin and cleanses from all unrighteousness.

13) SKEPTICISM (sarcasm) – Skepticism is generated by allowing sarcasm to feed and to take over our thoughts.

The definition of sarcasm is: ridicule or mockery used harshly, often crudely and contemptuously, for destructive purposes.

So many times we see in the media and among circles the mockery about the Bible, God, Jesus, etc. Jokes are shared among people to make fun of things and people that should be respected and never been mocked or ridiculed.

This mockery comes from the Devil, with the evil intention to twist the holy to common, the good into bad, the supernatural and beautiful into rational and undesirable.

The most difficult challenge we face today when sharing the Word of God is the spirit of skepticism that is in the world today. People simply doubt and challenge everything we say. The worse situation is even inside of so many churches, where faith for the supernatural to happen has been replaced with doubt and unbelief, making good preachers having to go into lengthy sermons and a lot of reasoning to prove that God is still alive and that He performs what He has promised.

Of course, it isn't difficult for us to identify the problems we are having to believe through one or more of the aspects of the "shell", described above. If you have identified that your faith has been hindered in one or more of the aspects defined above, pray specifically for that area of the "shell" to be broken and the core, the living faith to be released and to produce. Say out loud:

"I break and rebuke _____ (the specific area) in my life! I renounce it and don't want it to be a part of my life anymore! Get out of my heart and mind never to come back, in Jesus name! I am what the Bible tells me I am; I have what the Bible tells me I have; I believe in the Bible and eliminate from my life all the things that block my faith to be released now, in Jesus` name, amen!

CHAPTER 9

6th Requirement to enter the holy of holies:

A Heart Cleansed from A Bad Conscience

In the context of what the Bible teaches us about the conscience, we either have a lack of conscience or five other kinds: good, seared, bad, defiled(corrupted) and weak.

It is important for us to understand the differences between them, because they play important roles in our lives.

The conscience is the individual's sensibility as to what is right and what is wrong, especially based on the principles one was taught. For example: if a child is taught about the dangers of cocaine and the damages such habit may cause, a conscience will be developed in that child about this matter. If the child experiments with it, his/her conscience will "weigh upon" or "hurt" because it had already been taught about the cocaine and the addictive influence and damages it will cause in the mind and body.

The **lack of conscience** or unawareness is the lack of information about a subject or information that is not yet clear in the person's mind about that subject, defined as right or wrong, as expressed by David in Psalms 19:12:

"But who can discern his errors? Forgive my hidden faults".

Here, David was declaring that there are some things he did not clearly know to be right or wrong and is asking God to forgive him from hidden faults (which he had committed without knowing they were wrong in God's eyes).

The **good conscience**, mentioned in I Timothy 1:19:

"Holding on to faith and a good conscience, which some have rejected and so have suffered shipwreck with regard to the faith."

Good conscience is the one that was developed knowing basically what is right and wrong, but is also sensitive and opened to the Holy Spirit changing it, according to the teachings of the word of God. The good conscience is subject to being convicted if any sin is committed. So, after being convinced by the Holy Spirit of a sin, it shows repentance, which leads to confession and asking of forgiveness from God. It is good because it does not avoid the truth and because it is "bothered" by sin, quickly turning to the solution God has prepared for the problem, according to I John 1:9:

"If we confess our sins, he is faithful and just, and will forgive our sins and cleanse us from all unrighteousness".

A good conscience has a great conviction of the grace of God and His forgiveness and the right understanding of the power of the blood of Jesus shed on the cross, which was sufficient to pay for all of our transgressions.

The **seared** conscience is described in I Timothy 4:2B:

"...having their own conscience seared with a hot iron".

Searing or cauterization is a medical procedure done to close wounds and cuts with a hot metal. The seared or cauterized conscience is that which is closed to the operation and conviction of the Holy Spirit. This is the sin unto death because the conscience is closed and not open to be convicted of sin anymore. So, if isn't convinced by the Holy Spirit, it won't repent from sins and won't receive the forgiveness of God, the whole process is blocked. In the majority of cases, this is a process that started with the person lying to the conscience continuously, which leads to the conscience being changed to accepting behaviors that it didn't accept before. It is like the person that feels guilty when he/she tells a lie in the beginning, but after a while, makes telling a lie a habit after saying to his/her own conscience that this is normal, that everybody does it, the bible is old school, that we shouldn't be hard on ourselves, that we shouldn't be fanatic, times have changed, etc.

This is so serious, the bible teaches us that we shouldn't even pray for this sin, according to I John 5:16:

"If anyone sees his brother committing what is not a mortal sin, he will ask, and God will give him life for those whose sin is not mortal. ***There is sin which is mortal; I do not say that one is to pray for that****".*

The reason why we should not even pray for a sin which is mortal, it is because it is about an individual who remains in this sin, as explained in Hebrews 6: 4 through 8, which says:

*"For it is **impossible** for those who were once enlightened, and have tasted the heavenly gift, and have become partakers of the Holy Spirit, and have tasted the good word of God and the powers of the age to come, if they fall away, to renew them again to repentance, since they crucify again for themselves the Son of God, and put Him to an open shame. For the earth which drinks in the rain that often comes upon it, and bears herbs useful for those by whom it is cultivated, receives blessing from God; but if it bears thorns and briers, it is rejected and near to being cursed, whose end is to be burned".*

This word is very important and serious: "for it is impossible for them to be restored again to repentance"; it is a clear sign of a seared or cauterized conscience which can no longer be convicted by the Holy Spirit.

The seared or cauterized conscience is the result of having been systematically deceived, because when we lie to our own conscience, it lies back to us. The individual compromises principles and truths, allowing him/herself to be convinced that "it is not really like this" or "it has nothing to do with it", accepting practices and concepts that are contrary to the word of God and the moral standards, considering wrong things as being normal, gradually practicing them in his/her life.

A **bad conscience** is defined in I John 3:20:

*"Whenever our hearts **condemn us, greater is God than our hearts**, and he knows everything".*

A bad conscience is a conscience that identifies sin but goes into a self-condemnation mode, not accepting or believing it is possible for God to forgive it. It blames itself ruthlessly and is, most of the time, based on some frustration of an expectation the individual had about him/herself.

It is the case of the conscience of the individual that says: *"I will never do such a thing; I will never fall (or fall again) back into such sin".* Then, suddenly, by a trick or deceit of the devil, the individual ends up falling into that sin and the frustration and disappointment with him/herself is so strong that the individual keeps brooding over the problem, believing the accusations of the devil and saying to him/herself, *"how could I have done this? This is too much; how could I have committed such a mistake? What a horrible person I am! I do not deserve the forgiveness and love of God! I am not even going to pray anymore"!*

Let me say something I have learned in my life: have you noticed that when temptation comes things seem to be small? I have never heard anyone say, "I told a "big lie…"; on the contrary, it is always a "little lie". Have you ever heard someone say, "I am going to step outside to smoke a "big cigarette"? On the contrary, they always refer to it as a "small cigarette". I have never heard anyone say: "let's have a "big beer"? It is always a "small beer"! And so on and so forth: taking a "peek" (internet), "little stone" (crack), " just a little run" (cocaine), just a sip, etc., etc., etc. It is never a "long peek", a "big stone", a "long run"! This seems even funny, but it is true and hidden in all this is a strategy of the devil, that is, to allow the wrong things to seem so innocent, small and inoffensive, that doing them should cause no harm. But the thing is that this brings on something even more harmful: when someone falls into this trap and other temptations, the devil turns from being the tempter to being the accuser. He comes up with the accusation that turns that something that was so small into something horrible and big. He even says, *"do you still have the courage to pray?" "How can you still find the courage to go to church?" "Are you going to ask for forgiveness? God will not forgive your sin!" "You deserve to burn in hell!!!"* This creates a bad conscience, one that sees no possibility of forgiveness.

This danger is even greater when it involves someone who is a perfectionist. Perfectionism is different from seeking perfection, which is something Jesus tells us to seek in Matthew 5:48.

To perfectionists nothing is sufficiently good, they are always being critical of themselves because things did not happen the way they would like for them to, they are not doing their best, nothing will ever be the way they would like it to be, etc. This is very bad and it affects even their relationships and creates in such a person a permanent state of frustration and condemnation, even to the point of believing that God is not satisfied with what was accomplished. It also leads to a great danger, that is, the person begins to find fault in all things, people and situations. This is because the perfectionist becomes an idolater of his/her own reputation, always preoccupied with what others might think and they are afraid of disappointing others.

I John 3:21 and 22 says:

*"Beloved, if our hearts **do not** condemn us, we have confidence before God, and we receive from him whatever we ask him because we keep his commandments and do what pleases him".*

Our hearts need to be purified from a bad conscience because otherwise we will fall into condemnation, which leads to sadness, which leads to anguish, which leads to bitterness, and which will ultimately contaminate others, according to Hebrews 12:15.

Most people that have a bad conscience have a problem forgiving themselves. If we don't forgive ourselves, we are taking in a position as more righteous than God, because if He, who was the offended one is willing to forgive us, who are we to disagree with him and not forgive ourselves?

Another factor that creates a bad conscience is the lack of practice of very important virtues outlined in 2 Peter 1:5 - 8: Faith, goodness, knowledge, self-control, perseverance, godliness, mutual affection and love, which will cause to forgetting old sins, as recorded in 2 Peter 1:9:

"For whoever does not have these things is nearsighted and blind, forgetting that they have been cleansed from their past sins".

If you suffer from a bad conscience, it is important that you begin to truly believe in what the Bible teaches in I John 1:9:

"If we confess our sins, he is faithful and just, and will forgive us our sins and cleanse us from all unrighteousness".

By faith, start to declare, even if you are not feeling it, that you believe in the forgiveness of God and the power of the blood of his son, the Lord Jesus, to cleanse you from all sin. Thank Him, because the Lord is merciful and fulfills his word. Therefore, no longer accept the guilt and accusation of your faults and sins, because they have already been carried by Jesus, as it is written in Isaiah 53:5:

"But He was wounded for our transgressions, He was bruised for our iniquities; The chastisement for our peace was upon Him, and by His stripes we are healed.".

Isaiah 1:18 declares:

"Come now, and let us reason together," Says the Lord, "Though your sins are like scarlet, they shall be as white as snow; Though they are red like crimson, they shall be as wool".

This verse is in the old testament, before Jesus death in the cross. If that was possible in the old testament, how much more the blood of Jesus is able to regarding our sins, if we believe in the Father's mercy, grace and love?

A bad conscience is allied to the accuser and agrees with him, being self-condemning and neglecting the cleansing power of the blood of Jesus, the mercy and grace of God, which is His undeserved favor for us.

Receive now the peace that the forgiveness and the cleansing of sins bring to your heart.

The **defiled conscience** is that which sees sin and the devil in everything. Someone who has his/her conscience defiled keeps blaming and condemning him/herself for everything he/she and especially others say or do. This is very typical of religious and legalistic individuals. They confess to know God, but their lives show bitterness and frustration, which are not the characteristics of an individual who has the joy of salvation and the abundant life Jesus promised.

Paul also mentioned this type of attitude in Colossians 2:20 through 23:

"Therefore, if you died with Christ from the basic principles of the world, why, as though living in the world, do you subject yourselves to regulations: "Do not touch, do not taste, do not handle," which all concern things which perish with the using—according to the commandments and doctrines of men? These things indeed have an appearance of wisdom in self-imposed religion, false humility, and neglect of the body, but are of no value against the indulgence of the flesh."

The mistake is that the defiled conscience has the appearance of wisdom and devotion (see the last part of the verse), but it is of no value! It even gives the impression of spirituality but, in reality it is a pile of rules and regulations of the world.

Titus 1:15 and 16 declares:

"To the pure all things are pure, but to those who are defiled and unbelieving nothing is pure; but even their mind and <u>conscience are defiled</u>.

They profess to know God, but in works they deny Him, being abominable, disobedient, and disqualified for every good work".

The **weak conscience** is the one that was referred to in I Corinthians 8:11 and 12:

"And because of your knowledge shall the weak brother perish, for whom Christ died? But when you thus sin against the brethren, and wound their weak conscience, you sin against Christ".

The weak conscience is that of the individual who is not firm in his/her convictions and ends up being offended when seeing the brethren acting in a way that it is not clearly identified in the Bible as being right nor wrong. For example, some Christians drink wine and other alcoholic beverages, while others condemn this practice. This is one of the most controversial themes in the bible. If a brother who is weak and has a weak conscience sees another drinking, this could offend him/her. The word of exhortation the apostle Paul brings here means that it is better for us not to do some things that are doubtful, so as not to run the risk of offending a weak brother, than insisting on such practices and end up exposing that brother to the risk of being offended.

Now, that you have seen the kinds of conscience, you have the opportunity to have your heart cleansed from a bad conscience.

If you haven't forgiven yourself, you can do it now, by taking control of your own soul (mind and feelings) and decide to take the position of believing in the word of God and not in your own condemning conscience.

Believe in the power of the blood of Jesus and in the grace and mercy of God. He wants to renew and cleanse you. The peace that will reign in our hearts is wonderful and therapeutic when we are forgiven by God. All guilt and bad conscience are eliminated. A great relief envelops our being and there is the certainty that there is nothing pending, no question unresolved between us and God. The feeling we now begin to have is that of lightness and peace.

CHAPTER 10

7th Requirement to enter the holy of holies:

The Body Washed with Clean Water

"...and our bodies washed with pure water."

The word used here is "soma", which is used both for physical bodies as well as the body of Christ.

The Bible teaches us that we were made in three parts: spirit, soul and body. When we are born again, our spirit is like a baby that will mature. The spirit, which is the inner man has a body. Of course it is a spiritual body, as I Corinthians 15:44 declares:

"...If there is a physical body, there is also a spiritual body".

The bible doesn't give details about our spiritual body, but it shows that God also has a body, even though He is a Spirit, He has feet (Matthew 5:35), hands (Isaiah 59:1), eyes (Proverbs 15:3), mouth (Isaiah 40:5).

The only pure or clean water that exists spiritually speaking, is the Word of God that has the capacity of washing us spiritually, according to what Jesus said in John 15:3:

"You are already clean because of the word which I have spoken to you".

The Word of God acts efficiently in our being, removing the spots, dirt and impurities we have.

We must understand, however, what is being said. Our spirit is the one who understands the word "Rhema" (the revealed word) of God. It is not limited only to the "logos" which means the letter, that which has not yet been revealed, which is in the dimension of the natural understanding, according to what is in I Corinthians 2:14 through 16:

"But the natural man does not receive the things of the Spirit of God, for they are foolishness to him; nor can he know them, because they are spiritually discerned. But he who is spiritual judges all things, yet he himself is rightly judged by no one. For "who has known the mind of the Lord that he may instruct Him?" But we have the mind of Christ".

These verses clearly demonstrate that there are two levels of understanding the word of God: the natural understanding connected to the mind, the reason, and the spiritual understanding, connected to the inner man or the spirit. The revealed word is the one that penetrates the depth of our being because it was revealed by the Holy Spirit to our spirit and it is "engraved" within us.

This is the will of God, which was given to us through the new covenant, according to Hebrews 8:10:

"For this is the covenant that I will make with the house of Israel after those days, says the Lord: **I will put My laws in their mind and write them on their hearts;** *and I will be their God, and they shall be My people".*

This is the type of word that people lack the most in the churches and meetings and it is one of the major reasons they change churches or even quit going to any church. In reality, what holds the sheep in is not the fence, but rather the pasture.

The green pasture is what truly feeds. A lecture is not difficult to prepare and is the logos, something rational; but the revelation requires meditation in the word and a life of communion, fellowship with God by the person who is going to minister tthehe Word.

Therefore, the Word of God, like water, will only be effective in our spirit when it is able to perform the work for which it was sent. Like water, it is also able to penetrate the hidden places. In Isaiah 28:17, it is written:

"...The hail will sweep away the refuge of lies, and the waters will overflow the hiding place".

The Bible also assures us in Hebrews 4:12:

"For the word of God is living and active, sharper than any two-edged sword, piercing to the division of soul and spirit, of joints and marrow, **and discerning the thoughts and intentions of the heart".**

When we meditate in the word and we allow ourselves to be transformed by it, this washing process occurs. Therefore, it is necessary for us to open up in order for it to perform its work of cleansing.

When Jesus said, *"and you shall know the truth and the truth shall set you free"*, He did not mean that by reading the Bible alone or by memorizing verses of scripture, this would free us, but rather knowing the truth will. The root of the word "know", in the original, refers to intimacy, that is, to know the truth means to experience such intimacy and with it that our entire being is transformed, molded and cleaned by it.

We will know the truth, that is, the truth will penetrate our being and will pierce the shelter of lies, discerning our thoughts and the intentions of our hearts in such manner that it will free us from deceit, lies and wrongdoings, leading us to walk in its light, because the word of truth is:

"...a lamp to my feet, a light to my path". (Psalms 119:105)

Jeremiah 23:29 records what God says about his own Word:

"Is not my word like fire, says the Lord, and like a hammer which breaks the rock in pieces"?

The Word of God is so strong and firm that it is capable of breaking the strongholds created in us by the years of understanding and practice of deceit and lies.

What a wonderful gift God gave to us by giving his blessed and holy Word so that it can wash and transform us!

This is essential to our lives and for us to have a correct understanding. The Bible is not a pile of human rules and philosophies, but rather the living Word of God.

That is why the Apostle Paul declares in Romans 12:2:

"Do not be conformed to this world, but be transformed by the renewal of your mind, that you may prove what is the will of God, what is good and acceptable and perfect".

This transformation is something that occurs on a daily basis, when our mind is renewed by the knowledge of the truth and the old understanding is daily being replaced by the new one, point by point. This is the way through which we will walk in "newness of life", according to Romans 6:4.

This is where a lot of people get stuck and are stagnated in their spiritual life. They do not want to leave the comfort zone their mind offers, especially because any change brings a temporary discomfort, there is a certain apprehension when someone leaves the understanding they had with respect to something and replaces it with the revelation of the Word which will make them experience the good, pleasant and perfect will of God. Therefore, it is necessary to leave the "comfort zone".

This becomes a greater challenge for the ones that for a long time have acted and believed what they've learned and accepted through the years. Especially with respect to human traditions that were passed on from generation to generation, but that, in many aspects is not what God really wants them to practice and live by, according to the bible.

This is what is recorded in the book of Colossians 2:8:

"Beware lest anyone cheat you through philosophy and empty deceit, according to the tradition of men, according to the basic principles of the world, and not according to Christ."

The Apostle Paul declares in Ephesians 1:17 and 18, what is needed to get the revealed word, which is a spirit of wisdom and revelation and the eyes of our hearts enlightened:

"...that the God our Lord Jesus Christ, the Father of glory, may give you a spirit of wisdom and of revelation in the knowledge of him, having the eyes of your hearts enlightened, that you may know what is the hope to which he has called you, what are the riches of his glorious inheritance in the saints".

The Ephesians had been educated and taught human traditions and understanding, just like us, and only by God giving them the spirit of wisdom and revelation would they be able to know the hope of their vocation and take possession of the riches of the glory of their inheritance.

Leave your comfort zone and open your heart so that God may reveal his word, which will bring the knowledge of truth that will set you free, so that you may enjoy the riches of the glory of the inheritance of God in your life!

This is the bath that truly cleanses us from the dirt of deceit and frees us from the web of lies!

Experience the greatest and most marvelous "bath" you can ever have, which is that of being washed in the Word of God. Meditate on it, because all else will pass away, but the Word of God will never pass away. It is the truth that sets you free!

CHAPTER 11

Summary of the Requirements to Enter the Holy of Holies

If you have understood and are willing to take the steps and requirements to enter into the holy of holies, congratulations! Now it is time for you to marvel at the Shekinah of God.

So, in more practical ways, lets take the steps to enter into this wonderful place. Please, keep in mind that these are only suggestions, so don't see them as written in stone, but a guidance that was gathered after years of experience, mentioned here to help you:

1. Find a place where you can be comfortable, but not too comfortable so you may fall asleep. Make sure that there are no noises or other distractions that could hinder you or call your attention (maybe a soft and gentle praise song, playing at low volume will help);

2. Start praying in the spirit, according to I Corinthians 14:14 and 15.

3. Determine in your heart and your mind to boldly take the steps and enter the most holy place, disconnecting from all the thoughts and emotions that could create worries and anxieties;

4. Meditate on (pay attention and think about what you are reading), the Word of God, preferably in any book of the New Testament for 10 – 15 minutes;

5. Now, close your eyes and apply the blood of Jesus to the sins and mistakes the Holy Spirit will bring to your conscience, declaring: "the blood of Jesus purifies me of all unrighteousness, I've been forgiven";

6. After you feel that the burden and weight of sin has gone, take all your sicknesses, diseases, misfortunes, curses, weaknesses, lacks, miseries, illnesses, mistakes, wrong desires, perversions, compulsions, anguish, defeats, accusations, emotional sickness, rejections, works of darkness, mental illnesses, pains, bitterness, depression, negative arguments, lusts, works of the flesh, witchcraft, disturbances, oppressions, destruction, robbery and death, apply and see by faith all of them inserted in Jesus' flesh. Keep in mind that this is called the "new and living way", meaning that it is a dynamic process of transferring from your life to His flesh.

7. Check your heart and let the Lord search it, so no second intentions are present, making it difficult to worship the Lord in all sincerity. Make sure that no other interest other than devotion, gratitude and total surrender to Him is the real motivation of entering the most holy place;

8. Now, cast out all doubts and unbelief. Your heart has to have "full assurance of faith", so any "shell" or "bark" that is hindering your faith to be released has to be broken, allowing the DNA that is in the center of the grain of faith to come forth and produce the reality of entering the most holy place. The things of God are not mystical, but rather always depend on faith to be activated.

9. It is time to make your conscience clear and clean from all condemnation, knowing that the blood of Jesus is powerful

enough to cleanse us from all iniquities and sin we have committed. The price was paid in full, leaving nothing behind. Jesus declared in the cross: "it is finished", meaning that the whole work was done. Forgive yourself. The nature or the color of your sin doesn't matter, according to Isaiah 1:18 - "Come now, and let us reason together," Says the Lord, "Though your sins are like scarlet, they shall be as white as snow; Though they are red like crimson, they shall be as wool."

10. You have been washed by the Word, when you meditated on it. Your spiritual "body", or your inner man has been cleansed and you are ready to enter the most holy place.

11. Start visualizing yourself entering into this beautiful place of adoration and let your mouth express words in awe and admiration for the majesty and awesomeness of God, offering unto Him the sacrifice of praise, according to Hebrews 13:15: *"therefore by Him let us continually offer the sacrifice of praise to God, that is, the fruit of our lips, giving thanks to His name"*. With the spiritual eyes open and believing this place is real, according to Hebrews, enter into it and you will be surrounded by the Shekinah, the glory of the Lord, as it was in the past. It is real and marvelous. Its light is very strong and glorious; it brings the assurance that all is well and it brings overflowing peace. Our problems become very small in the presence of such majesty and brightness.

Additional considerations

There is no one like God. He is indescribable and absolutely awesome. When we enter into the holy of holies and we face the Shekinah, we are in such awe, that from our spirit emerges a great desire to worship God and to express to Him our admiration, respect, veneration, acknowledgement, gratitude and honor; to express how wonderful and perfect He is and how much He must be admired and reverenced. His attributes must be recognized and declared by us in a true attitude of humility and submission to Him. Words and declarations are made by us, towards His majesty. Words can start to pour out from your mouths, such as: "Holy, Holy, Holy is the Lord;" You, Lord, are clothed with strength; You reign and have dominion over all things and over the entire universe; nothing is hidden from your knowledge; everything is clear and evident to your eyes; everything and everyone is subject to your commands and principles". We open our mouths in admiration of Him and declare the wonderful and unparalleled characteristics of His being; His love, wisdom, mercy, sovereignty, power, authority, glory, justice, perfection, holiness, grace, integrity, forgiveness, kindness, longsuffering, compassion, patience, gentleness, beauty and uniqueness (there is none even similar to Him).

The Bible tells us that unity and harmony are characteristics of His reign; therefore, there are no fights, arguments, rebellions, strikes, competitions, betrayals, disdains, insults or cursing in His magnificent presence, but rather: respect and submission to the King of kings. His face is radiant and His heart beats for men; His gaze is the same as the one directed to Peter after the betrayal (of deepest purity and cleanliness).

Before Him we feel small and fully dependent on Him; all things and all glory are from Him, to Him and for Him, forever and ever; our spirit desires more of His presence and the grace that flows from His being. His magnificence is absolute; He is pure love; the base of His Throne is justice and judgment; the stability and strength of this reign is unshakable; its structure and action is eternal and consistent; there is a continuous celebration of the triumph of Jesus on the cross and His victory over the flesh, the world, darkness, sin, the devil, death and all evil; all attention is on the great King, from whom life, light, love, grace, wisdom, peace, happiness, joy, forgiveness, virtue, power, authority, understanding and purity flows; all is very transparent and there is no way to hide anything or anyone because the light penetrates everything and everyone, exposing even the most intimate parts of our being; there is an order for everything and nothing is made by vanity or without a clear purpose; everything is made for the benefit of all, where humility reveals total agreement with what is said and done by the great King; His joy overflows our being and becomes our strength; our words are few, but they are like the gold apple on a silver platter and ascend as a fragrance before the Father; we wish to leave all in order to spend eternity in this place; there is a desire within us for everyone to experience this; a desire is born to share with others about the SHEKINAH and how much joy and change it brings to us; it is impossible for us to enter into His presence and remain the same.

FINAL WORDS

It is in worship that we set our priorities in order, which means that, what really matters is not **us**, but **God**! He is the center of our lives; we adore Him; we acknowledge who He is; He has all the power; He deserves all the glory; we acknowledge His lordship, His majesty, His holiness; that all things are from Him, by Him and for Him; that He is worthy of receiving all the honor and glory; that He is wonderful, holy, righteous, loyal, true, good, glorious, magnificent, extraordinary, sovereign, perfect, wise, merciful, whole, compassionate, loving, great, unique, patient, powerful, excellent, living bread, alpha, omega, omnipresent, capable, sufficient, omniscient, strong, omnipotent, the best, the greatest, the most beautiful, the only one who is worthy of all glory and all honor!

Do you accept the call of Jesus to become a true worshiper? Do you wish to enter into the holy of holies, to experience the Shekinah and have the privilege of being molded in the image of our beloved savior?

May God bless you with the practice of what has been exposed in this book and may your life be transformed when you contemplate the face of the Lord, and, as it is written in I Chronicles 16:29:

"...*worship the Lord in the beauty of his holiness*".

ABOUT THE AUTHOR

Born and raised in an evangelical home, Helio Vassão Nespoli had his real experience of conversion in 1974, when he was 15 years old. This experience was so intense, that he felt a calling to preach and be a minister of the gospel. He was ordained a pastor in 1985 and started planting churches with his wife. Together, they've planted 7 churches both in the US and Brazil. They have 3 grown up kids and have been ministering in over 100 churches during their ministry. Pr. Nespoli understood that the majority of peoples' problems are due to a lack of a genuine relationship with God. The main purpose of his life and ministry is to teach people to walk in the Spirit. That is why he has developed a relationship with the Lord and in 2009 had the first experience of entering the most holy place and encountered the SHEKINAH. After that impacting experience, the Lord inspired him to write this book, which explains the steps to enter into the most holy place and experience the wonderful and glorious SHEKINAH.

www.ingramcontent.com/pod-product-compliance
Lightning Source LLC
Chambersburg PA
CBHW052108070526
44584CB00017B/2394